Harry N. Abrams, Inc.
Publishers, New York

By Jean E. Feinberg

with an Essay by
Peter H. Sauer

Wave Hill
Pictured

Photographs by
Lois Conner
Jan Groover
Stephen A. Scheer
and Philip Trager

Wave Hill Pictured

Celebration of a Garden

Project Director: Margaret L. Kaplan
Editor: Harriet Whelchel
Designer: Elissa Ichiyasu

This publication was made possible in part with funds from the
New York State Council on the Arts and CIBA-GEIGY. Wave Hill
receives public funds from the City of New York through the
Department of Cultural Affairs.

The Board of Directors of Wave Hill wish to thank Gilbert
Kerlin for his inspiration and leadership as the first Chairman of
Wave Hill. For twenty-five years, Gilbert Kerlin has set an
example of civic responsibility and generosity of spirit. This
book and all that Wave Hill offers today are the fruit of his
vision and an honor to his name.

Library of Congress Cataloging-in-Publication Data
Feinberg, Jean E.
Wave Hill pictured : celebration of a garden / Jean E. Feinberg:
with an essay by Peter H. Sauer ; photographs by Lois
Conner . . . [et al.].
p.   cm.
Includes index.
ISBN 0-8109-3954-1
1. Wave Hill (New York, N.Y.)—Pictorial works.
2. Wave Hill (New York, N.Y.)—History.
3. New York (N.Y.)—Description—1981—Views.
4. Photography—New York (N.Y.)—Landscapes.
I. Sauer, Peter H.
II. Conner, Lois.
III. Title.
F128.65.W35F46   1991
779'.36747275—dc20   90–47507

Published in 1991 by Harry N. Abrams, Incorporated, New York
A Times Mirror Company
Printed and bound in Japan

Contents

Wave Hill

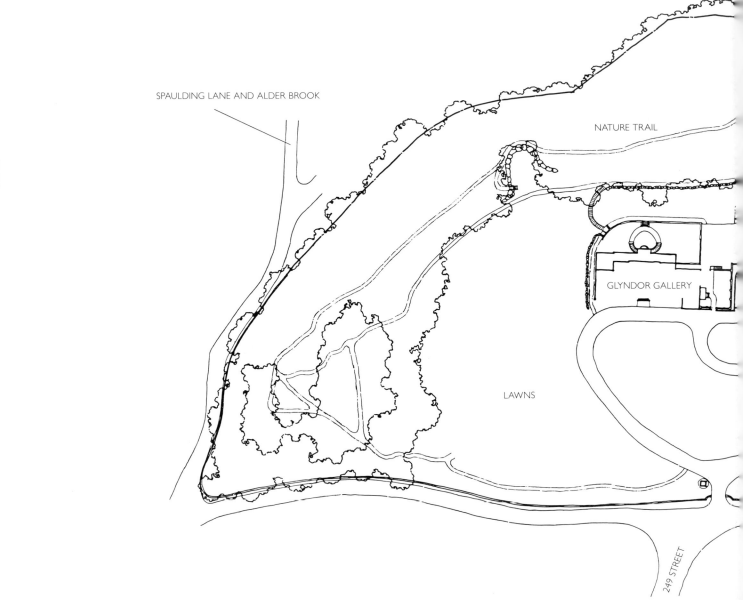

SPAULDING LANE AND ALDER BROOK

NATURE TRAIL

GLYNDOR GALLERY

LAWNS

N

249 STREET

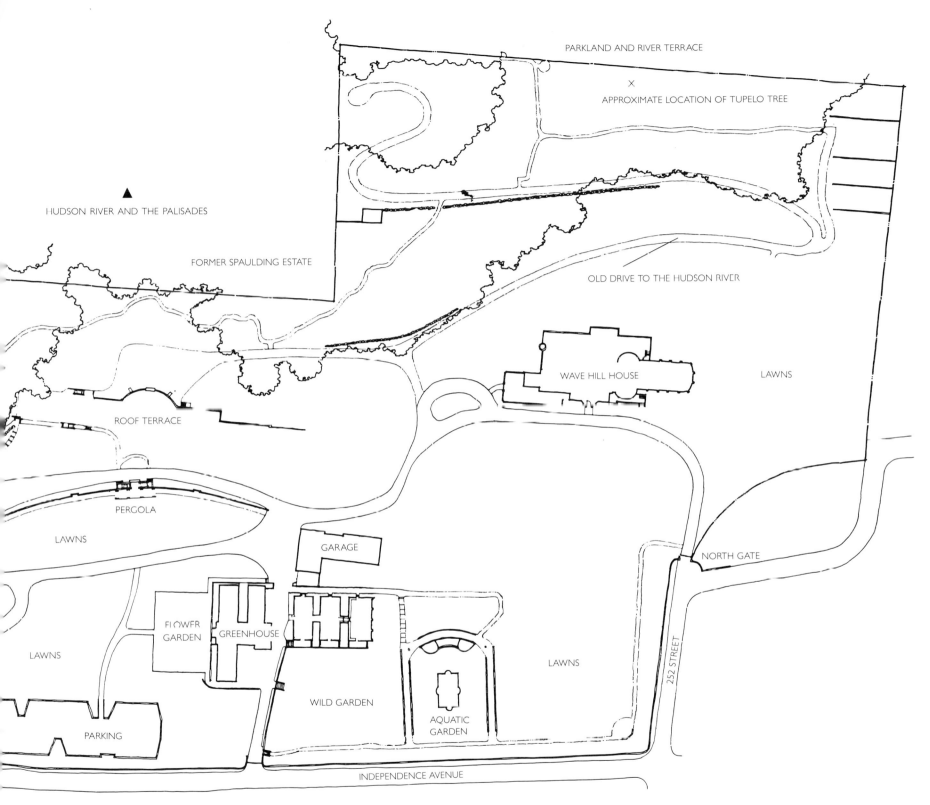

PARKLAND AND RIVER TERRACE

X
APPROXIMATE LOCATION OF TUPELO TREE

▲
HUDSON RIVER AND THE PALISADES

FORMER SPAULDING ESTATE

OLD DRIVE TO THE HUDSON RIVER

WAVE HILL HOUSE

LAWNS

ROOF TERRACE

PERGOLA

LAWNS

GARAGE

NORTH GATE

FLOWER GARDEN

GREENHOUSE

LAWNS

252 STREET

LAWNS

WILD GARDEN

LAWNS

PARKING

AQUATIC GARDEN

INDEPENDENCE AVENUE

Map art by H Plus

He to whom nature begins to reveal her open secrets
will feel an irresistible yearning for her most worthy
interpreter: art.

Goethe (1749–1832)

The Photographer's act is to see the outside world
precisely, with intelligence as well as sensuous insight.
The act of seeing sharpens the eye to an
unprecedented acuteness. He often sees swiftly an
entire scene that most people would pass unnoticed.
His vision is objective, primarily. His focus is on the
world, the scene, the subject, the detail. As he scans
his subject he sees as the lens sees, which differs from
human vision. Simultaneously he sees the end result,
which is to say he sees photographically.

Berenice Abbott, commenting on
Eugène Atget, 1964

It has come to this—that the lover of art is one, and
the lover of nature another, though true art is but an
expression of our love of nature. It is monstrous when
one cares but little about trees and much about
Corinthian columns, yet this is exceedingly common.

Henry Thoreau
October 9, 1857

Wave Hill is one of the New York metropolitan region's most cherished public spaces. Owned by the City of New York, it is unique among its many cultural institutions. Occupying a twenty-eight-acre site, Wave Hill stretches along the east ridge of the lower Hudson River across from an unspoiled section of the Palisades. This relatively small parcel of land has been a place of natural beauty for centuries; that it exists at the end of the twentieth century as an open, accessible site maintained as a public garden is close to miraculous.

The commissioning of photographs of Wave Hill began with a clear goal. The Wave Hill property was donated to the City of New York in 1960. After five years of interim care by the City's Parks Department, its management was turned over to Wave Hill, Inc. At that time an independent staff, which has grown over the years, was brought on board. Thus, since 1965 gardeners and other professionals have been at work, first to reverse the effects of a period of neglect, then to put into operation the changes and improvements needed to turn a private estate garden into a public one. In recent years the benefits of conscientious daily maintenance and long-term

planning have been particularly apparent. To date, a book on the gardens had not been published. The time was ripe to create one.

As a curator of contemporary art with an avocational interest in garden history, I was acutely aware of the pitfalls of most commercial garden pictures and the various publications in which they are included. Shelf space allocated for garden books has increased substantially in the last few years. With Post-Modernism's interest in color, decoration, and historic styles has come a burgeoning awareness of garden history and a revival in garden making as a potential component of both domestic and public landscapes. Books to feed this frenzied curiosity abound.

In studying the visual component of many garden publications, regardless of the merit of the text, one is struck by a disturbing fact: although the pictures may be of gardens from many countries, from different periods in history, and of radically different styles, they often show a monotonous homogeneity. I studied the pictures to learn what was specific and unique about each garden, but that information simply was not available through the visuals, even when the book or article was lavishly illustrated. There is a certain convention to

Preface and Acknowledgments

commercial garden photography that obliterates a garden's own design style. Thus, if the design of the Wave Hill garden and the aesthetic content of that particular place was to be "pictured" rather than obfuscated, a different approach from that seen in the ubiquitous coffee-table garden book seemed necessary.

Wave Hill has a history of first-rate exhibitions in the fields of contemporary art and American garden history, and it merited a publication in keeping with the quality and educational value of these programs. The goal was to communicate the nature of the site—and the landscape architecture and horticulture utilized therein—to transform Wave Hill into a garden of specific intent. To ensure the success of this goal, the nature of the photographs became a crucial issue. Rather than seek pictures to illustrate text, which is the accepted approach in most garden books, I decided to elevate the photographs to center stage. They would become the principal means by which the garden was explained. Photographers associated with fine arts, not commercial garden photography, would be called upon. Photography's visual language would be employed to interpret and reveal Wave Hill.

Once the project conception was firmly established, there was the curatorial task of artist selection. Which artists, individually and in relation to each other, would produce the aesthetically richest and most informative publication exhibition? Four photographers—Lois Conner, Jan Groover, Stephen A. Scheer, and Philip Trager—were selected and accepted the challenge of studying the gardens and taking a series of pictures. Each was given a free hand to adopt an approach consistent with his or her own philosophy of picture making. All came to this commission with an adventurous spirit, applying their complete artistic talents. They worked willingly over an extended period. They then patiently participated in the long production schedule demanded by a publication of this quality. Also, each in his or her own way taught me a great deal about garden design and contemporary photography. For that I am genuinely grateful. Thus, my first and most heartfelt acknowledgment is extended to these four individuals.

There are many members of the Wave Hill community who deserve mention for their role in making the complex undertaking of a commissioned photography book a reality. This project would have gone no further than being an ambitious idea if not for the initial support of the Wave Hill Board of Directors, in particular that of Gilbert Kerlin, Chairman until 1989, and David O. Beim, current Chairman and President. Mary Schmidt Campbell, Ex-Officio Board Member and Commissioner of New York City's Department of Cultural Affairs, also provided early encouragement.

The members of the Wave Hill staff deserving of special praise for the personal assistance they provided include Ann Arias, Renée Magnanti, and William Pangburn. Margaret W. Cowan and Eric Siegel were frequent sources of administrative aid. Other staff who have in various ways supported the arts at Wave Hill are Susan Antenen, Pearl Burns, Anthony Jennette, Susan Logan, Marilyn Oser, Chris Panos, and Earl L. Tucker. I also wish to thank Peter H. Sauer, Executive Director, for providing the essay on Wave Hill's evolution.

Many gardeners have cared for Wave Hill over the past decades. Those currently assisting Marco Polo Stufano, Director of Horticulture, and who are on a daily basis responsible for the gardens as portrayed here, are James Blase, Kevin Bost, Jose Concepcion, John Emmanuel, Madeleine Keeve, Eliza Reed, and Eric Swendseid.

Lois Conner would like to thank Grey Miller and Lisa Clifford for their assistance. Stephen A. Scheer would like to acknowledge Ned Gray for printing his color enlargements. Philip Trager would like to thank, as always, his wife, Ina Trager, and his assistant, Lisa Sanderson.

I am indebted to the staff of the Photography Study Center at The Museum of Modern Art, New York, for permitting me access to the Collection and Library, and to Leslie R. Close, former director of the Garden History Program at Wave Hill, for her collegiality and assistance in editing the photographs.

I particularly wish to thank Margaret Kaplan, my editor at Abrams, for supporting this project in concept, that is, before the pictures were taken, and for seeing that they were assembled into this beautiful volume.

Jean E. Feinberg
Curator and Director of Exhibitions
Wave Hill, March 1990

Wave Hill Pictured: The Landscape, The Garden, and Photography

One of the most popular and widely exhibited subjects in the history of photography is the landscape. It is a theme that spans the medium's one-hundred-fifty-year history. Landscape has been with us since the birth of photography, from William Henry Fox Talbot's earliest categorizations of photographic subjects to the present day as exemplified by Thomas Joshua Cooper's most recent pictures of the British Isles. To list all the significant figures in landscape photography who have worked in between is to survey the greatest names in photography. Dozens of the medium's most distinguished and accomplished members have turned their lenses outward to the landscape. An arbitrary list of the most well-respected landscape photographers may include the following names: from the mid-nineteenth century, Gustave Le Gray, Roger Fenton, Carleton Watkins, Timothy O'Sullivan, and William Henry Jackson; from the turn of the century and the early twentieth, Frederick H. Evans, Edward Steichen, Peter Henry Emerson, Thomas Frederick Goodall, and Alfred Stieglitz; from the first half of this century, Paul Strand, Edward Weston, Albert Renger-Patzsch, Imogen Cunningham, and Eugène Atget; later on, Ansel Adams, Minor White, Eliot Porter, Harry Callahan, Frederick Sommer, and Paul Caponigro; and, more recently, Lee Friedlander, Robert Adams, and Hamish Fulton.

In labeling pictures "landscapes," historians and photographers alike have allowed the term to have very broad meaning. It is indiscriminately applied to almost any outdoor subject. For this reason useful discussion, of necessity, requires limiting its definition. A first narrowing of meaning is put forth by John Szarkowski, curator of photography at The Museum of Modern Art, New York. He proposes to define a certain group of landscape pictures as those concerned with "the philosophical meaning of the natural site—those places where man's hegemony seems incomplete. . . . Landscape pictures . . . express an apprehension of the difference between our special human concerns and the earth's own compulsions."[1] Thus, landscape pictures become those that deal in some manner with the natural site. Falling under the umbrella of this definition in the United States are, first, the photographers who worked during the mid-nineteenth-century period of exploration, when, as Weston Naef has pointed out, there was a rise in "landscape consciousness" and "the appreciation of nature as a work of art."[2]

This interest in the natural site continued into the twentieth century and is now associated with those photographers who ventured into our national parks. This happened for an obvious reason: it was in the parks that natural sites might still be found. Even though parks have been photographed repeatedly by accomplished photographers, our western parks in particular continue to offer a special appeal to each generation of picture makers. They must search themselves for their own special relationship to what we have come to think of as *wilderness*—the untouched or pure landscape.

Once natural-site photography is set apart as a principal subgroup of landscape pictures, there is still the issue of how to meaningfully categorize and define all that remains. Given that the American populace set out to conquer its wilderness with astonishing speed, the number of landscape pictures that focus on something other than the natural site has with time logically increased and overtaken the wilderness picture. Setting aside the urban landscape as not relevant to our discussion, numerous categories of landscape still remain. These can be grouped into one class of pictures that I propose calling *working* landscapes,

where the terrain is altered and used for productive activities such as agriculture, and/or *built* landscapes, where there is significant structural alteration, such as the complete regrading and relandscaping of a parcel for the creation of a suburban development. All these landscapes exhibit the consequence of human intervention. Because the absence of human intervention is what characterizes wilderness, it is this factor that separates pictures of the worked or built landscape from natural-site photography.

The archive of American pictures of worked or built landscapes taken in this century is vast. Subjects span the continent—from rich farmland to poverty-stricken dust bowls, from small village greens to suburban backyards, from the environments surrounding elegant grain silos to those set in the shadow of the towers of nuclear power plants. Pictures of these types of landscapes have been recognized by historians as individually significant, yet a comprehensive history of landscape photography, in which all these picture types and the many others that belong to the working and built groups are included, has yet to be written.

Pertinent to our concern is realization that garden photography represents a specific type of landscape picture that depicts the worked

and/or built landscape. These specialized images are ill served when they are haphazardly grouped with other landscape pictures with which they have little in common. Garden photography merits consideration as a genre in its own right. If it is to be grouped with other landscape pictures, it ought to be with pictures that consider human interaction with the landscape. For example, garden photography may have a more meaningful relationship to certain types of social-landscape photography or architectural photography than to natural-site landscape pictures.

From the beginnings of photography, gardens have proffered themselves as a favorite subject. This is particularly true in Europe, where there has been a history of garden building and a history of the depiction of idyllic and pastoral landscapes in painting. Even a cursory glance at photographic history reveals dozens of images that merit inclusion in a catalogue of garden photography. Using the recent survey catalogue *The Art of Photography 1839–1989* as an arbitrary source, one can identify twenty pictures from this exhibition that easily fall into the genre of garden photography.[3] That this many pictures were culled from a volume organized thematically, yet one that did not include the garden as a photographic subject, is support for the significance of this unsung subject in the history of the medium.

Today, we understand that the age of true wilderness is long past; our attention, therefore, must turn to other land issues. In fact, in the realm of art, many are spiritually saddened rather than elevated by wilderness pictures. Once, a wilderness picture was a "metaphor for freedom and heroic aspiration";[4] now, it is more likely to serve as a metaphor for loss. Realistic environmentalists recognize that human intervention is not an option to be considered but a reality to be dealt with. There is no turning back the clock. The focus of current environmental activism is not on avoiding human intervention but on discovering how humankind can coexist with the planet in a nondestructive manner.

Gardens are cultural artifacts with aesthetic, social, and, at times, political content. They are among humanity's most positive reformations of the earth's surface. Garden building is a means for human beings to extend themselves into the landscape in a manner that preserves landscape values. The physical structure of a garden is created by contouring the ground plane and sculpting space and shapes out of plant materials. Successful gardens offer an environment that engenders communication with both the natural and the cultural, as gardens exemplify an interaction between the two. Garden making, therefore, can represent a human intervention with the landscape that glorifies rather than violates a strong land ethic, and garden photography has the ability to capture and visualize these impulses.

A spellbinding characteristic of Wave Hill is its expansive sky and the breadth of river view. It is what one notes first. Then, after taking in this grand vista, attention moves to a variety of garden rooms reached by pathways and lawns, many graced with prize trees. As if these built and carefully tended places of horticultural splendor are not enough to satiate the garden lover, Wave Hill also provides several greenhouses full of specimens available for study and delectation. The visitor walking through this landscape cannot help but be impressed by Wave Hill's abundance.

In addition to the open views, the sweeping lawns, and the garden enclosures, Wave Hill has a forest garden. Half of the property is dedicated to this natural-style environment. The forest fills the western edge, and through it loops a meandering trail that takes the more adventurous garden lover on a journey through native woodland habitats.

What every visitor to Wave Hill grasps immediately is that here the natural and the cultural harmoniously coexist. The built world venerates what existed prior to human intervention. Visitors, most of whom are from urban environments, know that Wave Hill and its environs are not wilderness, and that a visit to Wave Hill will not provide answers to complex ecological issues. But a visit does serve a valuable educational function. Through a direct experience with a landscape such as Wave Hill, one in which an aesthetic sensibility has been put to work, one comes away with a positive and crystal-clear notion concerning how we can positively interact with, build upon, and simultaneously preserve our landscape. Although there may be great confusion in how to deal with our environmental problems, there is no confusion about the value of Wave Hill and its existence as a stellar example of human culture's ability to preserve a land ethic in the midst of the most intense urban development.

It is perhaps our current disbelief in man's ability to create beautiful landscapes that causes the average garden visitor to attribute natural properties to built spaces. Visitors resist the notion that the shape of a hillside that seems so perfect has been created by moving earth. They think a fifty-year-old tree just happened to grow in that spot, rarely considering the possibility that it reflects the foresight of a prior gardener. It is hard for visitors to accept that the shape, color, and texture of a herbaceous border were worked out in detail, and that the state in which the border now flourishes evolved through several cycles of careful revision.

Given the scarcity of wilderness that still remains and its inaccessibility for those living in highly developed regions, it is very important to recognize the positive role humankind can play in shaping landscapes. We must acknowledge that, like the wilderness, built landscapes should be valued not for their potential usability but for their aesthetic and spiritual value. Gardens are environments that, despite their artifice, connect us to the natural world and a powerful landscape ethic.

In this last decade of the twentieth century, Wave Hill offers itself as a subject of great value. For Lois Conner, Jan Groover, Stephen A. Scheer, and Philip Trager to photograph Wave Hill is an optimistic and intelligent act. Each, in his or her own way, has understood it

as a combination of a site with natural environmental properties and one that demonstrates the highest form of aesthetically motivated human intervention.

Although the history of garden photography has yet to be recorded, serious scholarship has been devoted to the greatest of all garden photographers, Eugène Atget (1857–1927). A four-volume catalogue, *The Work of Atget,* and a series of related exhibitions at The Museum of Modern Art during the early 1980s were produced by John Szarkowski and Maria Morris Hambourg. Through them, one of the basic concerns that underlies and is shared by Atget's photographic career and the work produced by Conner, Groover, Scheer, and Trager at Wave Hill is addressed: the photograph as a document.

Before The Museum of Modern Art exhibitions, there was the mistaken conception of Atget as primarily an architectural photographer. Because this picture type had made its way into public collections and had been accessible and visible, it was better known than his other subjects. Now, it is clear that Atget was the greatest documenter of the worked and built landscape—the parks, gardens, and

rural countryside of Paris and its environs. Atget studied certain places in detail, among them many gardens, returning repeatedly, sometimes one day after another, or in other instances with great lapses between visits. We know also that some views are consistent, and others, when compared, display great variations. This change may be due to simple shifts in atmospheric conditions, a different placement of the camera or major developmental changes in the photographer's intent.[5]

These changes in both the described form and philosophical content of pictures of the same or similar locations raise the question of what it means to call Atget's work documentary.

There is at the heart of Atget's work a profound paradox. The premise on which the work was based and the function to which it aspired depend on our acceptance of the objective reality of the past: we are to believe that these facts are not only true but significant, that each picture refers to events that were part of the meaningful narrative that we call history. And yet the pictures themselves, the means by which this past is reported to us, are formed not in accordance with disinterested and repeatable rules, but according to the mysterious promptings of an individual sensibility. The photographs in fact insist on demonstrating their own historical capriciousness by showing us that an ancient tree or stone wall is never twice the same, and by delighting us with the recognition of this anarchistic truth.[6]

None of the four photographers—Lois Conner, Jan Groover, Stephen A. Scheer, and Philip Trager—who came to photograph Wave Hill is considered a documentary photographer. Nevertheless, they were invited to create a body of work that records a garden as it currently exists, the pictures to serve future generations as documents of how the garden looked at a previous time.

Clearly, we are presented with four distinctly different visions. The contradictory nature of these visions calls into question the documentary usefulness of the pictures. Our inclination, to declare that this publication captures the reality that is Wave Hill, is brought into doubt. Fortunately, through this doubt, caused by a mix of "historic fact" and "individual sensibility," we are led to Szarkowski's "anarchistic truth." Nothing is seen twice by one pair of eyes as being the same. Nothing is perceived by two sets of eyes as originally identical. And the camera intervenes with its own set of visual propositions. It is through the filter of an art-

ist's aesthetic that the Wave Hill pictures have come into being. Each photographer elected to picture what he or she considered significant. Interpretation superseded record making.

Each photographer invents his or her own reality. This reality, however, is directly tied to and derived from first-hand experience of a place. When four visions are presented side by side, as in this volume, viewers are forced to recognize the subjective nature of their own vision. By this process, they are given the opportunity to evaluate its limits. For those open to expanding their own perceptions, this knowledge is exhilarating.

In a recent article, writer Tim Davis laments the fact that professional landscape historians are not looking at what he calls art photography, that is, at pictures by artists such as Conner, Groover, Scheer, and Trager. All too frequently the landscape specialist uses illustrative pictures of the poorest quality as source material and evidence, relying on these pictures as the key to significant data, accepting information purveyed therein at face value without understanding how pictures function. Analysis of landscape would benefit, Davis states, by turning away from what Steichen labeled "tweedle-dee and tweedle-dum photographs"

to those of Steichen's professional colleagues. Through the images of the creative photographers, we are given interpretive material about the landscape, the same type of information that the landscape historian seeks.

Creative photographers have paralleled and perhaps even preceded academic landscape analysts in their investigation of the evolving American landscape. . . . Both the cultural geographer and the photographer of the cultural landscape seek to make the unobserved visible, to understand the complexities of the human landscape. . . . Like the phenomenologists, the photographer seeks to discover the significant details that reveal the essence of a place . . . the ability to convey both the particular and the general aspects of human experience is the key to the distinction between poetic photographs and the more common illustrative variety that accompany most landscape texts.[7]

This advice from Davis will, I hope, serve to counteract the argument that the subjective and interpretive nature of Conner, Groover, Scheer, and Trager's pictures has been pushed to such an extreme that their informational value, particularly to landscape scholars, has been lost. To consider the illustrative as objective, and therefore informative, and the stylized as so subjective as to be worthless is naive. For what one historian views as objective may in truth be equally stylized but merely conventional. And what is recognized as radical and unusual may be loaded with information revealed through the image's eccentricity.

Bonded implicitly within the photographers' personal essays on the Wave Hill environment are their own ideas about what constitutes a good photograph as well as invaluable information about the built landscape before them. From this interwoven language of form and content comes a revelation of facts and ideas about the formal design, landscape ethic, and cultural content within the garden named Wave Hill.

Lois Conner (born 1951) came to

Wave Hill with far-reaching experience in photographing both the garden and the landscape. She is the one photographer of the four commissioned to photograph Wave Hill who previously had been associated almost exclusively with outdoor subject matter. Conner began photographing the landscape early in her career. At first it was one subject among many;

by the late seventies, she declared landscape to be her subject of choice.

Conner came slowly to a professional commitment to photography, although she first took the camera in hand at an early age. When she was nine years old, her father, an electrical engineer, gave her not the typical Brownie but a 2¼" camera.[8] He taught her how to make her own contact prints, so from the start she understood the laboratory to be explicitly tied to the process of picture making. Throughout high school she pursued this avocation in her home environment of rural Pennsylvania. She studied photography formally at the University of Delaware, working now with a 35-mm camera. She had entered college with the intention of majoring in art, which meant a combined study of art history and studio work, but after two years she decided that fashion design was more to her liking. In 1971 she arrived in New York City, her home base ever since, to study at The New School and the Fashion Institute of Technology. Although her attention shifted to fashion design, she maintained an involvement with photography, for fashion is strongly tied to the photographic image. During this period she met Philippe Halsman, a *Life* magazine photographer. Largely due to his advocacy, Conner

abandoned fashion and made the commitment to photography. In 1975 Conner concluded her undergraduate wanderings with two years of photographic study at Pratt Institute. After a break from formal education, in 1979 Conner returned to academia by enrolling in the graduate photography program at Yale University, from which she received her M.F.A. in 1981.

Because Conner's years of higher education span from her entrance into the University of Delaware in 1969 to her graduation from Yale in 1981, they do not form a compact era separated from other life activities. Interwoven with her formal schooling is the creation of a body of work that dates from 1974 forward.

In the early 1970s Conner was a frequent visitor to The Museum of Modern Art, assiduously studying the prints on view from the permanent collection. Her eye was attracted to the late-nineteenth and early-twentieth-century platinum prints by Pictorialists and Photo-Secessionists such as Frederick H. Evans, Peter Henry Emerson, Edward Steichen, and Alfred Stieglitz. Also during this period, she met Richard Benson, who would later become her teacher at Yale. He showed her platinum prints by Tina Modotti that he was developing. In 1974 Conner switched from a 35-mm camera to a larger format 5 × 7" camera and began experimenting with the platinum process. Until 1980 she worked in both platinum and silver. Since then she has worked exclusively in platinum.[9]

Conner prefers large negatives and makes prints only of their equivalent size. When she works, as she did at Wave Hill, with a 7 × 17" Banquet camera and an 8 × 10" Deardorff, her negatives and exhibition prints are 7 × 17" or 8 × 10", respectively. Thus, Conner attests, everything captured on the negative will appear in the final picture. With enlargements and with silver printing, Conner felt, this was never the case. Technically, in a silver print the silver crystals are suspended in a gelatin emulsion that sits on the paper surface; with platinum printing, the platinum is actually bonded to the fibers of the paper. This bonding, combined with the inherent color difference between silver and platinum and the kind of delicate tissue papers that Conner uses with the latter process, yields in her view a greater consistency between what she sees through the lens and what is captured on film.

The other formative aspect of Conner's development, outside of her formal schooling, was her work at the United Nations. From 1971 through 1983 she was employed there in a variety of full- and part-time clerical and administrative positions. She also did graphic design work and made documentary architectural pictures. The significance of her United Nations experience lay not in the actual jobs assigned to her but in the impact of the time spent in this international atmosphere, and especially in the opportunities for travel that it offered. In 1975, under U.N. auspices, she left the United States for the first time. She set out not for Western Europe, as most Americans do on their first foreign excursion, but to the Ivory Coast in West Africa. For three months each year, from 1978 through 1983, she was assigned to Geneva. From these experiences Conner was smitten with wanderlust. At first this entailed a simple urge to explore foreign lands; by the mid-eighties, though, it had become a compulsion tied to her working process. Lengthy trips of exploration and discovery during which she often walks and bicycles great distances have become her modus operandi. Her travel is designed exclusively for the purpose of studying a place and photographing it. Conner extended her stays in Geneva by traveling in Europe before and after her Swiss assignment. She received a Guggenheim Foundation Award in 1984 to travel to China, to which she returned in 1986 and again in 1988. Within a fifteen-year period, Conner photographed in West Africa, Switzerland, France, Germany, England, Burma, Thailand, China, Tibet, and Turkey. This insatiable appetite for travel, particularly to places unblemished by the modern era, connects Conner with such great travel photographers of the mid-nineteenth century as Frances Frith, Felice A. Beato, and John Thomson.

Once Conner had her M.F.A. and was able to teach, she left the United Nations. The adjunct positions she has filled since then are important in that they have facilitated her American travel. In the same way she ventured out from Geneva to make pictures, Conner has utilized teaching stints away from New York as a means of seeing and photographing this country. The geography of her American pictures includes examples from Arizona, Utah, New Mexico, California, Washington, Hawaii, and Louisiana as well as her original home state of Pennsylvania and her adopted one, New York.

Conner's wanderlust, the criterion she uses in selecting her destinations, and her switch to the platinum process are tied to the development of landscape as her exclusive subject. Conner had always photographed the landscape of rural Pennsylvania, but from 1975 to 1979 landscape yielded to an interest in portraiture. In the late seventies this interest waned and her attention again became riveted on the landscape. Conner attests that although she altered her theme, she maintained the eye of a portraitist. Her trees became the sitters—living entities that were silent, motionless subjects, directly facing the camera and dominating the picture frame. Gradually, this head-on portrait approach gave way to a broader view of the landscape in the woodland and farm country of Pennsylvania, the Indian territory, and the national parks of the American Southwest as well as in the gardens and parks of Western Europe and China.[10]

It is difficult to engage Conner in a discussion of the differences among the landscapes she pictures. She avoids talking about the varied character of the wilderness landscapes, working landscapes, social landscapes, urban landscapes, and public parks and gardens that she has photographed. She considers all of the outdoors grist for the landscape mill. In studying Conner's oeuvre, though, it becomes apparent that she favors landscapes that have been tamed in

Lois Conner. Untitled (Hampstead Heath, England). 1983. Platinum print

Lois Conner. Untitled (Hangzhou, China). 1984. Platinum print

some way by society yet that retain an affinity for the natural. Wilderness as defined in the natural-site photography of Ansel Adams and Eliot Porter holds only minor interest for her. Nor do landscapes that are overbuilt or scarred engage her. She is attracted to a rhythmic order, preferring a quiet grace to the grand or baroque.

Wave Hill presented itself as a perfect Conner subject. She approached the commission as a travel experience. Even though her trips, from February through December of 1989, were daily ones, her visits produced the same kind of adrenalin rush as had her lengthy trips abroad. For Conner, unfamiliarity is an essential ingredient in exoticism. Having never been to Wave Hill, she was presented with a totally new landscape experience. Once she entered the grounds, she might as well have been a thousand rather than fifteen miles away from midtown Manhattan.

At first, the newness and aesthetic richness of Wave Hill were mesmerizing. The potential for pictures was everywhere. She walked and studied the site with great care, exploring all twenty-eight acres. In time, the garden seemed to diminish in size; many initial images were discarded, but the potential for great pictures continued as seasonal and daily fluctuations offered constant variations. Of the four photographers, Conner took the broadest view, literally covering the greatest ground.

Conner describes her approach to Wave Hill—her approach to most landscapes—as essentially narrative. She considers our visual experience of a place to be derived from the steady movement of our head and eyes from left to right. This is a continuous reading of space, a surveying motion on an even plane. The landscape is not absorbed through a staccato juxtaposition of isolated images; rather, it is a continuous flowing composition she equates with Chinese scroll painting. The scroll is a lengthy horizontal picture, which one reads by slowly unscrolling with one hand and simultaneously rescrolling with the other. Conner shares with John Szarkowski the opinion that one of the primary tasks of good picture making is deciding when to stop scrolling—to permit a right and left border to be created—thereby stopping the flow and creating a limited, framed composition. "The central act of photography, the act of choosing and eliminating, forces a concentration on the picture edge—the line that separates in from out—and on the shapes that are created by it."[11]

Conner recognizes that in this essential photographic act of framing, the continuous narrative of the scroll painting is violated and that it is in the detail or the fragment, and not in an assembling of elements, that truth lies. The photographer ought to "isolate the fragment, document it, and by so doing claim for it some special significance, a meaning which [goes] beyond simple description."[12] Nevertheless, Conner adheres strongly to the belief that just because she, as a picture maker, must select details of the landscape that she frames in her viewfinder, she need not consequently deny the narrative experience. This is particularly true for the Wave Hill pictures. Here, a strong horizontal presence carries forth through the flow of the river, the sweep of the Palisades, and our narrow north-to-south boundaries. Conner set out to preserve this given, not to work against it.

For this reason, the majority of her Wave Hill pictures were taken with a Banquet camera, which produces a 7 × 17" negative. The horizontal emphasis of these images accentuates a left-to-right narrative reading and description of the depicted space. Conner considers the 7 × 17" pictures to be panoramic,

although both her camera and lens are stationary.

One of Conner's Wave Hill pictures that readily fits into the conventional concept of panorama is plate 1. This picture captures the physical heart of Wave Hill, a primary location from which paths radiate outward. Every amateur and commercial photographer who comes to Wave Hill attempts this core picture: an overall descriptive view that documents the horizontal sweep of the site. Most photographers face the river straight on and are defeated by it. Brilliantly, Conner turns her back. She faces east, toward the garden and Riverdale proper, rather than west, i.e., into the same section of the garden but with the Hudson in the background. Both perspectives give us the entry path, fragments of the central lawns, the principal Flower Garden, and a partial view of the greenhouse complex, but Conner's version adds as backdrop a curtain of large trees, some situated on Wave Hill ground, others "borrowed" from adjacent residential properties. The Banquet camera captures the visual sweep of the garden, taking in a view that is both wider and in greater detail than the human eye is capable of; yet, as a picture on a page or one hanging on a gallery wall, it unfolds as most visitors' principal conception of the archetypal Wave Hill view.

Another panoramic picture utilizing this expansive compositional format also depicts a primary, open space—the north lawn (plate 15). Because of its grade change, the sweep of this lawn is impossible for the visitor to take in through a single visual survey. One has to reconstruct the entire lawn view in the mind's eye after walking over and through it. Conner photographed the lawn from a nearby rooftop, creating a picture that visitors who have explored the lawn recognize and assume they have seen before. Actually, through Conner's panoramic picture they are seeing the large lawn as a single image for the first time.

The richness of the image in plate 1 is so great that Conner was driven to explore its content in greater depth. In plate 2 she moves in closer, framing the central portion. This picture is still essentially panoramic, in that a large area is being surveyed. In plate 3 Conner puts the 7 × 17″ format to use for a different compositional treatment as she now zeroes in on a small space within the Flower Garden. Here the horizontality of the image is not about a panoramic sweep of the eye; instead, it is used to maximize the movement of our

eye as it accumulates the magnitude of minutiae available for visual delectation. The 7 × 17″ format accentuates the unfolding nature of this material—the density of plant life and the complexity of its organization. The viewer has not stepped back to survey a scene; on the contrary, the viewer's presence within the space is palpable. We become the visitor, standing in the unseen but felt foreground, within inches of touching the glorious hibiscus in the picture's upper left corner.

These two compositional approaches—descriptive overviews of the terrain and close-up examinations of the horticulture—guide Conner through Wave Hill. Because of the variety to which she turns her lens, these two tactics never strike us as obvious or redundant. For example, plates 13 and 14 present sections of the gardens populated with trees, shrubs, ground covering, and the views they offer into adjacent lawns. Plates 10 and 11 focus on plant detail, illuminating isolated fragments of the garden environment.

There are at Wave Hill an excellent tree collection and many fine, large shrubs. Given Conner's prior interest in photographing trees, it is not surprising that she elected to study them at Wave Hill. Conner favored trees and

shrubs that offered a linear emphasis (plates 17 and 19), as well as those with massive silhouettes (plate 18). For this reason she preferred deciduous trees that had lost their leaves, or the section of a tree or shrub where an unusual trunk (plate 11) or clean lower extremities dominated (plate 9). In the details of trees, Conner cut off the top of the plant, capturing the juncture of tree with earth. By exploiting her 7 × 17″ format, she emphasizes the plant's horizontal outreach, the manner in which the branches reach out from the trunk or the roots spread through the earth. All of Conner's tree portraits convey the plant as having a life force, being connected to the earth and stretching outward into the landscape.

What Conner has taken as her literal subject, that which she has elected to frame and describe, is fundamentally secondary to what she has done photographically to these views. She interprets her subject by exploiting opportunities offered by the photographic process. The elements and design of the Wave Hill garden that she describes on film—its trees, flowers, lawns—are presented within a thick, subjective atmosphere. She layers the garden structure with greater content, evoking feelings about the place as a living environment with a particular character and enveloping mood.

Conner's commitment to the platinum process plays a significant role in the achievement of specific atmospheric effects. Always drawn to black-and-white photography, Conner, like many of her colleagues, claims not to see the world in color. For her, color is overtly seductive, leeching away full photographic potential. The range between pure, bright white and darkest black, both of which she avoids, is inclusive, and the platinum process offers her a means to explore this range. Through it, she has become a master of tonal variation.

Two of Conner's great achievements in the Wave Hill pictures are her depictions of different light and air conditions as both still and moving. To accomplish this she uses to full advantage her mastery of tone, yielding a soft, cushioned world with no jarring movement or juxtapositions, no hard edges or austerity of any kind. When she first began working at Wave Hill, she preferred visiting the gardens on quiet, still days. She saw wind as a problem, interfering with her desire to present the landscape as the equivalent of a motionless sitter. She followed the weather reports, anxiously hoping for the early morning temperature changes that might produce fog or haze. These weather conditions would augment the creation of a soft atmosphere, necessitating a print with a middle range of tones.

After spending time at Wave Hill, Conner set aside her original predilections and began working with the weather as she found it. Still preferring early morning over midday, she discovered the potential in bright morning sunlight (plate 4). She also worked with the wind. Instead of avoiding it, she granted it center stage (plate 8).

In picturing Wave Hill, one of Conner's primary achievements is an interchange of the material and immaterial. She gives the immaterial substance and dissolves form into unseen forces. In her pictures, air becomes palpable. One can see it, touch it, smell its bouquet. It is not the empty negative space that surrounds the positive and physical. When the air is light and soft, it adds as much delicacy and texture to the picture as the specimens that fill the flower beds or the early blossoms on spring shrubs (plate 14). When the air is thick and dense, its weight is enough to counterbalance that of the most stately tree trunk (plate 18).

If the air carries brilliant light and strong wind, it has the power to dissolve the forms it touches. The summer sunlight obscures the articulated structure of the Japanese maple in plate 2. Shaking branches and fluttering leaves are more than just that; the blur of their form, depicted with subtle distinctiveness because of Conner's extraordinary articulation of tone, becomes the equivalent of the wind itself. The heaviest limb is reduced to a shimmering haze (plate 8). Through light and wind, contour and silhouette are obliterated.

Whether Conner pictures the immaterial as palpable or dissolves form into an embodiment of natural forces, her goal remains the same: to illustrate the predominance of atmosphere. Even though she describes the topography and the horticulture, her chief subject is the enveloping role of the physical environment. The drama of winter's grayest clouds rolling down the Hudson, the summer sun streaking across the lawn, or the wind's effect on the underside of a branch are what Conner captures and communicates with her Banquet camera and delicate printing process. She understands the power of the environment and how its atmosphere overtakes you the moment you enter the garden. For Conner, it is what gives the landscape its character, and it is therefore what she elects to give visual form.

Philip Trager (born 1935) is recognized as an architectural photographer. In the early 1980s, through two bodies of work—a commissioned study of the campus of Wesleyan University in Middletown, Connecticut, and an acclaimed survey of the villas of Andrea Palladio—he expanded the scope of his architectural vocabulary. Previously, his work had emphasized the purity of the edifice; with the campus and villa pictures, he shifted to architecture as it related to site. These experiences of photographing architecture within a landscape context set the stage for Trager's venture into the gardens of Wave Hill.

Trager settled into photography slowly and cautiously. Like many in this age of popular photography, he was given a camera, as a thirteen-year-old, using it first for amusement and then, in his late teens, for modest financial ventures. He reluctantly confesses to preparing accident reports for attorneys. During college at Wesleyan, he continued to take pictures, but on his own time, as there were no studio or history of photography courses offered. He stopped photographing while in law school and avoided picking up a camera during his early years of practice, although he now admits that the desire to do so was present. In 1966

Trager recommenced taking pictures, at first casually but finally in intense competition with his law practice. By the late 1960s Trager was seriously involved with photography, and today he pursues it with a vengeance so intense one assumes he is striving to make up for lost time.

Trager began by taking pictures close to his home in Fairfield, Connecticut, first a simple portrait of a friend in the woods and then a series of pictures of that yet undeveloped countryside. From the start he worked with a view camera, taking it with him on holidays to the American West and Southwest. Totally ignorant at this point of the history of photography—a gap in his education that he has since filled—he unknowingly approached the same subjects as others had before him. The Southwest pictures include Trager's first building studies. Among the structures his eye elected to photograph is the well-known church Rancho de Taos in New Mexico. Trager continued on occasion to photograph architecture, but these early pictures were interspersed with other subjects, in particular an ongoing portrait series of his wife, Ina.

By the mid-seventies, Trager had arrived at the working method he employs today. After careful consideration, he selects a subject that

entails photographing a large number of buildings. He pursues that one subject with a vigorous appetite until he is visually satiated. The resulting group of pictures represents an in-depth study, which he then publishes in book form. Although he does exhibit the pictures, his intention is more to produce what one could call a *modern album* than a show's worth of pictures, which is the working impetus of many artists. His first book project was a three-year study of Connecticut architecture, published in 1977.[13] It contained sixty photographs of buildings in his home state. The architecture dated from around 1692 to 1968, and his building selection was wide-ranging. The pictures, however, were all decidedly straightforward, with an emphasis on full-frame facades. In these photographs, the facade becomes the building's literal face, the purveyor of its history and character.

Through the Connecticut project Trager was totally seduced by the potential of architecture; his next step was to venture over the state line into New York, specifically to Manhattan. Working over a three-year period, he produced the eighty-eight pictures that comprise *Philip Trager: New York*. These pictures—less individual portraits of isolated buildings, as was the case with the Connecticut project, and more portraits of the cityscape—include a variety of perspectives on buildings as they merge within the context of the dense, urban grid. The written comments accompanying the locations list at the end of the book are a telling statement regarding his intent in photographing the fast-changing Manhattan skyline. "The views shown in these photographs were selected on aesthetic grounds; that many of the buildings shown may be architecturally significant is, in truth, accidental, for architectural importance was not the photographer's primary concern. The following identifications are provided merely to satisfy the curiosity of the interested reader."[14] Ironically, the volume, merely ten years old, has already taken on a documentary value as several of the buildings and streetscapes no longer exist.

Trager returned to his home state and his alma mater, Wesleyan University, in 1981. The ensuing book, *Wesleyan Photographs,* is definitely a portrait of a place rather than a series of individual building pictures, and as such it marks Trager's stylistic turning point. Trager communicated the character of the one-hundred-fifty-year-old university environment by highlighting the interaction between the

grounds through which the students walked and the buildings in which they studied. Trager often opted to frame and emphasize architectural details rather than present large views. Light- and shadow-filled fragments exist as moments in time. The small volume communicates and connects to an alumnus's memory of a place recast with a modernist eye. This content gives it significance beyond that of a volume documenting the campus's distinguished architecture.

Trager's next project and the one with which he is most frequently associated is a comprehensive study of Palladian architecture, known through the beautiful volume *The Villas of Palladio: Photographs by Philip Trager.* The book contains eighty-nine pictures covering twenty-one villas, taken during a series of trips between 1984 and 1986. Palladio's villas, which are set into the gently rolling hillsides of the Veneto, were designed in proportion to their site, extending out into and merging with their agrarian surroundings. Appropriately, Trager's Palladian pictures emphasized the relationship between the villas and the landscape in which they so sensitively reside. Distance views place the buildings in the landscape, and numerous details emphasize the juxtaposition between

building parts and particular plants or dramatic vistas. Seen in its totality, Trager's Palladio album frames one of the most accomplished and influential Renaissance architects in a modern light. Palladian building vocabulary and proportions are seen anew, as is the brilliance of his siting. For architectural historians, it is a revealing and breathtaking study.

With the Palladian survey behind him Trager was looking for a new venture. He had recently declined an offer to document a group of Frank Lloyd Wright buildings. He was considering a new subject, dancers in the landscape—a body of work he has since pursued. That however was a warm-weather-only undertaking.[15] The timing of the invitation to work at Wave Hill was just right, as Trager was eager to turn his attention elsewhere. The Wave Hill book offered both a subject and format consistent with his methods and interests.

Trager's photographs of Wave Hill fall into three basic groups: a series of greenhouse pictures, images of the Wild Garden, and a group of essentially lawn views. Of Trager's twenty pictures included in this volume, nine are of the greenhouse complex and its immediate surroundings. Of the three buildings at Wave Hill—Glyndor, Wave Hill House, and the

greenhouse—the greenhouse is the architectural feature most aligned with the garden. His approach to this series is similar to that which guided his pictorial essays on Palladio's Villa Almerico Capra (La Rotonda) or the Villa Godi. In those series, Trager does provide the viewer with close-up shots of the facade but almost because it is obligatory. How can an architectural photographer deny a front elevation view? However, this frontal perspective, which dominated his Connecticut work fifteen years earlier, has been replaced by a more complex understanding of what constitutes a building's character, especially one functionally and structurally tied to its site.

Trager now approaches his subject like an animal stalking his prey. He slowly circles round and round, observing the greenhouse from every possible angle. The results are pictures taken from unusual vantage points—an assortment of unlikely detail views that emphasize the building as it relates to the larger environment. There is a tradition of such detailed documentation in architectural photography. In his essay for the landmark exhibition *Photogra-*

Philip Trager. *Villa Almerico Capra (La Rotonda)*. 1984. Silver print *phy and Architecture 1839–1939*, Richard Pare points out the value of pictures of building details in comparison to overviews, and he offers, as an excellent example, Jean-Louis Henri Le Secq's portfolio of Chartres cathedral. Of Le Secq's twenty-five plates, only one approaches the church from a distance. It is through a series of details, rather than through overviews from a few angles, that the whole is best revealed.[16]

The first greenhouse picture, plate 21, is Trager's one required frontal view of the facade. This picture places the greenhouse complex within Wave Hill as a whole. It is seen as a group of low-lying structures nestled within the gentle slope of the hillside. Trager permits the stately elm before the greenhouse to dominate to such an extent that this picture becomes as much a portrait of this extraordinary tree as a record of a building.

Trager's angle of approach—a straight, head-on view of the facade—appears to make perfect sense. In actuality, however, it is a vision not readily apparent to the visitor. This perspective and those in many of Trager's other Wave Hill pictures are never the most obvious. They are not the ones available from the paths that regulate the pedestrian's experience—the

views that dominate the frequent visitor's general impression of Wave Hill. Nor are Trager's angles of approach at one with the intended pictorial efforts of the gardeners. In fact, Trager's pictures capture vantage points that will take the regular visitor by surprise, more so than anyone scanning the pictures in this volume who has never been to Wave Hill can realize.

Trager accentuates the transparency of the center house, a structural fact that merges the building and the landscape (plates 22 and 23). The greenhouse is completely integrated with the dramatic sky and river view. Greenhouses, with their glazing, are by definition the building discipline's most immaterial edifices, but the extent to which Trager has exploited this property is exceptional, a testimony to his understanding of this particular architectural form's photographic potential.

Trager continues to use his understanding of architectural form and its photographic possibilities as he moves in closer, at ground level, to the greenhouse. The west and east wings of the conservatory are whitewashed at certain times of year. In plate 28 Trager juxtaposes the transparent center house and the shadow of the previously seen elm that falls upon it with

Philip Trager. *Villa Godi.* 1984. Silver print

the opaque roof of the west wing. In plate 24 the east wing is a solid, impenetrable structure while in plate 25 the bright light shining through creates a delicate silhouette of the collection on view inside.

As Trager moves around the greenhouse, drawing our attention to the effects of changing light and shifting vantage points, the spotlight is shared with the Flower Garden that is its forecourt (plates 26 and 28), the foundation plantings (plate 24), and the seasonal beds of changing displays (plate 25). The greenhouse vies for attention, in plate 24 with the pine that commands the picture's middle ground, in plate 28 with the junipers as well as the densely planted beds in the picture's foreground, and in plate 26 with the simple tripod stake. In the picture of one of the greenhouse complex's outbuildings, the garage—a structure until this point ignored by photographers as unworthy—Trager has managed to capture, in the aftermath of a winter storm, the competitive yet essentially symbiotic relationship between landscape and architecture (plate 29).

Trager's pursuit of atypical vantage points and emphasis on the garden's connection to the larger landscape continues in his four pictures in the Wild Garden. The Wild Garden is a small, contained space in comparison to the greenhouse complex; nevertheless, Trager sought perspectives that would open it up and intertwine it with the rest of Wave Hill. Instead of looking into the space, the attitude of most photographers, Trager elected to look out from it. In plate 33 one looks out over the bare-branched sumac toward the river. From this perspective the drama of the sky is played out over the Palisades. By occupying two-thirds of the picture's space, it assumes a leading role. In plate 30, and moving in closer through plate 31, Trager embraces the Wild Garden with the stately trees that make up its border or that are actually situated beyond its boundaries. This puts the Wild Garden in context rather than portraying it as a separate garden room, lifted out of its isolation from Wave Hill as a whole.

In his third group of pictures, Trager looks out across lawns at the structural elements that exist in relationship to them, elements such as the pergola, very large trees, or vine-covered walls. Trager approaches the pergola and its adjacent lawn, with a temporary sunken courtyard sited there by artist Robert Irwin,[17] as he has other architectural features. First, there is the frontal shot (plate 34), an elevation view of the pergola, with an emphasis not on the structure itself but on the context in which it exists. This consists of the courtyard's granite steps, its sod interior that stretches out before them, and the densely clouded heavens that reach upward. In the second picture of the pergola (plate 35), Trager does not move in directly for a detail picture. This would be visually repetitive of the overview. Instead, he radically turns his camera angle so as to deny the structure's symmetry, the commanding feature of the elevation view. Now one side of the pillars is bathed in sunlight while another is cast in shadow. They are the strong vertical elements that span the distance between ground and sky. Trager's image emphasizes the many varieties and textures in the simple foundation plantings. Through his unusual angle, he is able to maintain a glimpse of the lower, forested ridge, the river, the Palisades, and the sky beyond.

Wave Hill is fortunate in having several large, old, and very grand beech trees. In two images—a distant shot of the beech in full foliage (plate 37) and a detail view of the lower trunk (plate 36) in which the original swollen graft mark dominates—Trager juxtaposes the contradictory states of the bulk and scale of this massive form, its huge umbrella of foliage, and its thick elephantine trunks and roots with the intangible immateriality of shadow and the dappled pattern of light created by the strong sun. Through photography these physical contradictions possess equal visual weight and informational value; together, they communicate the essence of one of the garden's most commanding elements. Maria Morris Hambourg has made similar observations in her study of an Atget photograph, also of a beech tree.

When he confronted the beech . . . Atget saw the shadow not so much as a pattern, but as the significant surrogate for the tree's ramification. . . . Atget gave condensed form to this idea: the trunk and adherent shadow are seemingly indivisible; they represent the whole tree both in substance and insubstantial aspect.[18]

Similar debts to and shared intentions with Atget[19] can be seen in Trager's view of the sweeping northwest and south lawns. Hambourg has pointed out that Atget, through his work at Versailles, came to understand that "hedges and trees as dark masses could greatly alter the spatial and expressive organization of the picture."[20] Trager makes use of this device in his approach to both of these lawns. In plate

39 he alters our perception of the lawn: its grade, its size, and its relationship to the adjacent area. What we perceive, due to his gathering of a line of trees from both the Wave Hill property and what lies beyond, is a very large, long lawn that rises only slightly as it extends for an undetermined distance. It is the lawn of a grand-scale park dotted and bordered with the mass of huge trees. In reality, the lawn's grade change is dramatic and its length relatively short. Placing the camera at a low point, Trager has shot into the hillside in such a way as to flatten and extend the slope. Trees only a short distance away now become plantings in a far distant background.

Trager has similarly manipulated the space in plate 40 by juxtaposing the darkness of an ivy-covered wall and nearby dense forest with the lighter tones of the soft lawn. By allowing the lawn this dramatic change in tone, its curve and depth are exaggerated. The lawn becomes a diagonal sweep from foreground to middle ground. As in plate 39, the adjacent landscape, here the ridge of the Palisades, is so neatly integrated into the picture that the boundaries of Wave Hill are obliterated. Again, Wave Hill has become a grand park, with a scale and size way beyond its modest twenty-eight acres.

This brings us to the issue of Trager's overall interpretation, or more to the point, his reinterpretation of Wave Hill. Trager was impressed with what he described as the "circumscribed world" of Wave Hill. This response to Wave Hill as a self-contained space that encompassed him as he worked was an overriding factor in determining his sense of place. For Trager, more than the garden itself, it was the natural environment—what I have described previously as its spellbinding characteristic, its expansive sky and the breadth of river view—that appealed to him. Everywhere Trager looked he found his eye drawn upward toward the sky, outward into the distance, or downward along its slope leading to the river. The garden was not to be looked into but out from. It was always linked to the larger, natural environment.

Circumscribed was never translated into signifying small. For Trager, circumscribed meant being separated from the oppression of the urban metropolis and the nearby suburban homes of Riverdale. Circumscribed meant being cushioned and enveloped by masses of billowing clouds, curtains of grand trees, and the wall of stone that is the Palisades. Therefore, in many of his pictures Trager places major emphasis upon the surrounding world, seeing Wave Hill primarily as a place within this context. As Trager moved around Wave Hill he was not led by the design of the garden itself. For him, locations to be photographed were noncontiguous, distinct places of visual interest. What links spaces and what gives many of his individual pictures relationship is the emphasis upon what he considers to be Wave Hill's unifying theme: the form-giving properties of the the sky and its light and the ever-present slope of the hillside as it descends toward the river.

Trager treats the garden itself, the forms that he incorporates into a larger environment—what garden-design professionals call landscape architecture—in a highly subjective manner. For Trager this terminology is particularly apt. Landscape architecture is the disciplined use of plant materials as building blocks in the creation of landscape, comparable to the architect's use of stone, concrete, and steel in constructing buildings.

Because Trager has been studying and photographing architecture for some fifteen years, he came to Wave Hill with an understanding of the place as a *built* environment. Often the visitors' clarity of vision is clouded by their emotional response to a place of beauty. Their grasp of the environment as man-made is obscured by their linkage of gardening with natural processes. Trager's architectural background prevents him from falling into this trap. His vision of the garden as landscape architecture—a built and structural environment designed with skill and knowledge of the plant world and the aesthetic potential therein—is crystal clear.

Trager draws our attention to the structure of the garden through the imposition of classical order and symmetry. He utilizes the properties of his medium, all that the camera and darkroom have to offer, to arrange the elements that comprise the landscape and to give them an order and precision not readily apparent to the unaided eye. Trager focuses on the largest elements in the landscape, ones that stand out and are often geometric in shape, and places them in the center of his picture. They function like the facade of a well-proportioned building. Everything takes its cue from them, be it the conical trees in the side view of the greenhouse in plate 22, the thin cypress on the hillside of the Wild Garden in plate 32, or the ovoid shrub along the greenhouse wall in plate 31. Trager utilizes these plants as mid-composition focal points. The structure of the Wild Garden is altered when we focus, not on the horticulture within its dense, complex beds outlined by circuitous paths, but on a single linear element silhouetted in the middle ground or the rhythmic line of the regularly shaped evergreens. Since the pictures are neatly ordered around central elements, so the landscape appears to be as well.

The emphasis on classical order is equally obvious in Trager's picturing of architecture, illustrating again his similar approach to plant forms and architectural ones. Not only is the roof of the greenhouse's center court placed within the picture's center, but its metal ribbing is read as a dominating grid (plate 23). Seen from another vantage point (plate 25), the triangular shape of the end of the west house is neatly juxtaposed with a trapezoidal perspective on the center court. The classical order of this picture dominates even though the architectural elements are only a backdrop for the brilliantly lit, Victorian-style planting bed in the photograph's foreground.

In speaking of his architectural work, Trager makes his photographic concerns very clear. He is not a documenter and he is not preoccupied with the architect's own intentions. His work is never literal; no effort is made to duplicate what the eye may see. Using his lens and his masterful darkroom skills, he creates a picture filtered through his own feelings and aesthetic response to a structure. The same can be said of his garden pictures. At Wave Hill, Trager waited patiently for the atmospheric conditions that would create the maximum drama, augmenting the role of nature as an element in any outdoor experience. He focused on the elements within the garden that offered the greatest stature and elegance, elevating their presence and role and declaring them the true stars of any great garden environment. They became the building blocks of the landscape and so merited individual attention and respect.

From an art-historical vantage point, Trager appears to have combined contradictory styles. His photographs merge the sweeping drama and grandeur of the baroque with the reasoned order and geometry of the classical. Within his landscape the grand gesture and the loud voice are present, yet not as unbridled energy. Overwhelming beauty does unleash emotions, but they are held in check by the structuring of the environment. Through this successful balancing act, Trager has created an inspiring vision of Wave Hill in which the overpowering drama of the natural world is held in place by the ordered beauty of the built environment.

Jan Groover (born 1943) was approached during the earliest stage of this project, before Wave Hill had a commitment from a publisher and when the scope of the project was still undefined. This was not a deterrent for Groover. She had heard of Wave Hill but had never been there. Plans were made for an immediate visit so she could walk the grounds and evaluate a potential subject. Just a few days after she explored Wave Hill for the first time, she was back with her camera, eager to begin.

Groover is an intense, hard worker whose first love is picture making, with picture viewing running a close second. She is receptive to the idea of photographing many things. This is not to imply she is not discriminating but to say that her enthusiasm in taking pictures comes from the fact that she recognizes the potential for visual interest as omnipresent. With this awareness she need not travel great distances to find compelling landscapes. The mere half-hour ride from her lower Manhattan home to Wave Hill seemed just about right.

Of the four photographers included in this volume, Groover is the best known, the recipient of critical praise and professional recognition. She has been exhibiting regularly in galleries and museums in the United States and Europe since 1974. In 1983 the Neuberger Museum, at the State University of New York in Purchase, organized the first comprehensive survey of her work. This was followed in 1987 by a retrospective at The Museum of Modern Art.

Jan Groover's New York gallery exhibitions of the last ten years have featured her still-life photography; consequently, she is often labeled exclusively as a still-life photographer. It is logical that this impression would take hold as critical writing focuses on what is most available and most recently seen. What is fresh from the studio is reflective of the artist's most pressing concerns. Through it artists are categorized.

A more careful review of her early work and an in-depth knowledge of her production of the eighties reveal Groover's approach to subject matter as more catholic than previously has been understood. She has a long history of working out-of-doors, in general, and an affinity to landscape, in particular. The Wave Hill

Jan Groover. Untitled (#937 New Jersey). 1981.
Palladium print

pictures are a distinct body of work, but they are not, as those who classify her only as a still-life photographer will incorrectly assume, inconsistent with her photographic history and philosophy.

Groover's biography is well known, having been outlined in the Neuberger Museum and MoMA catalogues as well as in miscellaneous essays. Much has been made of her background as a painter, perhaps too much; this emphasis on Groover's debt to painting is a reflection of the art community's lingering prejudice against photography as a primary medium with a visual language of its own. In 1965 Groover did receive a B.F.A. in painting from the Pratt Institute. Immediately thereafter she began teaching in the public schools of Plainfield, New Jersey. This is where she grew up and it remains a place she visits frequently. Groover returned to school to obtain, in 1970, a master's degree in art education from Ohio State University. Over the years she has maintained a strong commitment to teaching. For her it has never been a stopgap measure. She considers teaching to be an honorable profession and an invaluable learning tool for the serious working artist. After Ohio and until 1973 she taught painting at the University of

Hartford in Connecticut. In 1973 she moved to New York City, which has remained her home to date. Since 1979 she has been on the faculty of the State University of New York at Purchase. It was during her years in Hartford that Groover began experimenting with photography. Her first solo exhibition was in 1974 at Manhattan's Light Gallery, a now-historic location in that decade's push for the recognition of photography.

Groover talks easily about the chronology of her work. She groups what she has produced in two basic ways. The first revolves around her technical approach or working method and how it has changed. The second categorizes work according to the genre or the general subject matter to which these techniques have been applied. From this come the following groupings: from 1972 to 1975, color triptychs of cars and trucks taken with a stationary camera; from 1975 to 1977, color triptychs of urban and suburban architecture created by shifting the camera for each frame; from 1978 to 1981, color still lifes known as the *Kitchen Series;* beginning in 1979, but principally from June 1980 to mid-1983, landscapes, cityscapes, portraits, domestic scenes, and still lifes in platinum-palladium; from 1982 to 1986, tabletop still lifes with a narrowing of the scale of the surface, in silver; fall 1986 to the present, color still lifes; and fall 1987 to January 1989, color landscapes at Wave Hill. Groover also mentions, as grist for the mill, that in most summers during the past decade—in particular in 1989 after the Wave Hill experience she took black-and-white landscape pictures in New Jersey.

Critical discussion usually divides Groover's work into two larger and less revealing groups: the triptychs from 1972 to 1977 and the still lifes beginning in 1978. The triptychs are formal, conceptual pieces that investigate the camera's potential for both capturing and calling into question our reading of so-called reality. Groover set up a camera on the side of the road and photographed moving vehicles. She joined two or three frames, exhibiting these studies as diptychs or triptychs. Later, she allowed herself to move the camera around a site, still investigating a single location, though now concerned, not with how objects moving through it affected perception of the location, but how the shifting camera position more radically altered our reading of the place.

Once Groover turned from the triptychs to the single-image still lifes, her work was per-

ceived as moving away from issues connected with contemporary art of the 1970s and entering into a dialogue with the history of photography. In 1978 she jumped into a historic context by taking on photography's most common genres: the still life, the landscape, and the portrait. Her approach to composition, which often reflected historical precedents, was offered as a challenge to such photographic heroes as Weston, Strand, and Stieglitz.

Through Groover's evolution from an analytical, conceptual approach to one concerned with participating in and advancing photographic history through historically rich, straight subject matter, she increased the significant value of her own subjects' aesthetic impact. Bluntly stated, the merit of the truck pictures existed largely through the ideas they investigated. To arouse an aesthetic and pictorial interest in street signs and speeding trucks per se was not Groover's intent. With the still lifes, her concerns are radically different. Through kitchen utensils, plants, and fruits tumbling into the shallow space of the kitchen sink, and later displayed on tabletops, a mental as well as an emotional response is triggered. The beauty and sensuality transmitted by the arrangement of common objects is visually captivating. While

Jan Groover. Untitled (#1930 New Jersey). 1989. Palladium print

previously the ideas contained in the picture dominated, now the intellectual intent is balanced by a visceral response to an image's fundamental aesthetic quality.

It is pertinent to the discussion of Groover at Wave Hill to recognize just when this balance between the conceptual and aesthetic intention specifically began. Susan Kismaric points out that it took place at the end of the triptych series:

Once she realized she could continue the multiple-image work and move the camera, the original conceptual superstructure was relaxed. Groover's increasing responsiveness to the particular qualities of the subject before her rather than the manipulation of abstract space emerges in the pictures done for the bicentennial project,[21] but is not fully developed. . . . The resolution of the problem is demonstrated in her next series of pictures made in suburban New Jersey. . . . Groover's work to this point was more about form than sense of place. In her previous pictures things photographed were considered objects to be exploited for their color and form. In the suburban New Jersey photographs, Groover's ability to use the descriptive power of photography matured. The form and content of these pictures are consonant and indivisible.[22]

The last pictures in the triptych series were of suburban landscapes. They were taken on familiar territory, a terrain to which she was personally attached and for which she had particular feelings. Photographing in this setting brought issues into play that were not present when she had placed her camera arbitrarily alongside a highway. Now the character of the place, as much as what she was doing with her camera, became important. Her pictorial investigation expanded beyond spatial conceptualization. The viewer was given more information than before about the subject portrayed, and this subject was the character of a type of landscape.

Of the four photographers, Jan Groover spent the most time, over the longest period—making numerous visits from fall 1987 through winter 1989—at Wave Hill. This happened not only because she and Trager were invited to participate before Conner and Scheer but also because of her desire to mine her subject fully. She worked principally with an 8 × 10″ and a 2¼ × 4½″ camera. The twenty plates included here were edited from nearly two hundred and fifty photographs.

Even though Groover produced a large number of pictures, she confined herself to a small working area. After exploring the entire landscape on her initial tour, she began inside the greenhouse, photographing the plant collections on display. After several days of shooting indoors she moved outside, using the greenhouse complex as a radial point from which she moved only slightly outward. Groover returned again and again to the same or nearby sites, working serially in a manner that is not totally apparent from the twenty culled pictures included here. This focus on particular locations, shooting from only slightly modified angles under different daily or seasonal conditions, relates Groover's approach to Wave Hill to that employed for her outdoor triptychs.

Groover was intrigued by a short, gravel-covered walkway and its immediate environs. She photographed it again and again, utilizing the path itself as a strong compositional element, a line moving from foreground to background neatly dividing the picture (plates 41 and 42). The division of the picture by the path accentuates the difference between the garden space to its right and left. Both sides are graced with unusual trees. In the left foreground is a saucer magnolia. In its middle ground is a sugar maple. On the opposite side, in the foreground, is a Japanese umbrella pine and in the distance an American elm. Beneath the trees, on the left is grass while on the right there is a variety of dense ground covers. At first glance, the pictures of this area might each be interpreted as diptychs: two separate places linked by the artist but not actually existing side by side. This association with a variation on Groover's earlier formal technique comes about because in a single frame she has emphasized a disjunction in the landscape. If we are walking on the path and looking to the right we take in one view of a particular world; if we swivel our neck just slightly to glance left, we find another world entirely. By slicing the composition so emphatically with the pathway, Groover has brought this radical difference between two adjacent landscapes into the forefront of our visual consciousness.

The visual variety that this very small space affords is dramatically presented by a comparison between the scene taken during different seasons. Plate 41 was shot during the heat of the summer. We can feel the weight of muggy air as a hazy light rakes across the leaves of the magnolia and falls on the trunk of the pine. The light turns the leaves yellow and the pine a glowing red. Plate 42 was taken on a cold winter day, under blue skies and clear, sparkling light. Groover has moved back a few feet so that, instead of cutting off and fragmenting the magnolia, its structure is in full view. Groover makes the most of its complex, gangling form, its every twisting, linear detail visible in the clear winter light. By contrast, the space to the right of the path falls within the shadow of trees, not physically included in the picture but ostensibly behind the photographer. The shadows provide this side of the picture with a dark, mysterious overcast, shading the tree trunks, branches, and evergreens that compose the space.

At first, both pictures of this pathway provide a clear vision. The brilliance of the light and the sharpness of the imagery seduce viewers into believing they are accurately absorbing this place in its every detail. The pattern of the bare branches is sharply delineated. The shape of the pine's multiple trunks is precisely silhouetted. Nevertheless, our initial assurance subsides. Underlying this first impression is the reality that Groover has done her utmost to select an extremely complex location, one that she deliberately presents in the most confounding way possible. Her selection from the infinite possibilities that Wave Hill affords is deliberate, and the way this discrete space is presented does not allow us to come away feeling confident with our knowledge of this area of the garden, but we respect its chameleon-like complexity.

Groover applies this serial approach to Wave Hill's Wild Garden, the small garden space within Wave Hill that is one of its most magnificent. From a horticultural standpoint the Wild Garden is complex. Every square inch of ground space is covered with plantings, interrupted only by meandering narrow paths. Within this dense growth there is not only quantity but variety, so that color, texture, shape, and scale are constantly changing. The horticulture staff's goal is to create the look of a *natural* landscape rather than a formal, ordered one—hence, the name Wild Garden. The effort required to simulate this effect is great, as the gardeners must work vigilantly to hold this type of design in check.

Groover was cognizant of the effort that went into maintaining the design of the Wild Garden. She watched the gardeners at work and witnessed the result of their labor. However, what attracted her to this space was not the human effort that went into controlling the landscape and the fashioning of plants into a design that emulates the shape of nature's own plan but those moments when the effort for control was thwarted by nature itself. She sought to locate within the space those places where chaos and confusion prevailed. And if that confusion was not extreme enough to the naked eye, she used her camera to augment as much as possible this feature of disorder.

The Wild Garden is an intense place with an extraordinary abundance of visual material. The slightest shift in glance yields a different picture. Even the narrow paths are overgrown. There is little air, no breathing room.

Most photographers who take pictures of the Wild Garden fail to capture the quality of being in that dense space of a garden room. They shoot overviews, mistakenly assuming that this descriptive viewpoint is the best way to capture its essence. Groover's compositional acumen made her realize that sweeping overall views of the Wild Garden eliminate such crucial information. Empty foreground and open skies provide visual relief from the cacophony of plant life. Thus in plates 43 through 50, Groover's eight horizontal pictures of the Wild Garden, she eschews an overview, descriptive approach in which the space is given a context and relationship to neighboring areas.

In all of Groover's horizontal Wild Garden pictures she cuts off the foreground and eliminates the sky. Using a composition reminiscent of her still lifes, she compresses and intensifies the space, which becomes shallow and loaded, almost claustrophobic. Groover also uses a device that again recalls the diptych: she allows strong vertical elements to divide the space, thus confounding our effort to comprehend comfortably the way the space is organized. The planting beds are continuous, running into each other without separation. This garden space is impenetrable. We stand on the outside looking in at its unruly design.

In emphasizing the intensity and pictorial complexity of the Wild Garden pictures, it would be a mistake to neglect the obvious: these are frankly beautiful pictures of a beautiful place. Groover knows she is treading in aesthetically dangerous waters in dealing with this inherent attribute of gardens. Beauty can sabotage a picture's pictorial interest. In this series of images, Groover has succeeded in achieving pictures of great beauty that also maintain their identity as interesting and commanding photographs. We are delighted with the dancing daylilies in plate 50 and the spritely, ornamental onions in plate 47. We cannot help but gasp at

the fiery orange in the fall sumac in plate 46 or the dark purple of the Boston ivy in plate 48. Their glory and magnificence are a joy to behold and Groover relishes capturing this on film. But we are not allowed to languish for long before we are brought up short and made to work through the pictorial complexity of which the garden's abundance is a part.

Any garden, but particularly one such as the Wild Garden, affords a sensuous experience. Not only is our visual field gloriously abundant, but this visual feast also commingles with intoxicating garden sounds, smells, and textures. For some, this sensual assault is almost too much. One approach is to seek relief through order. The gardener does this by moving toward a more formal design. The photographer (as we have just seen in the work of Trager) may do so by imposing order within the picture. To Groover's credit, the success of her Wild Garden pictures is attributable in part to the fact that she does not shy away from the sensory assault of the garden but imparts it to us with full force.

Although Groover's experience at Wave Hill focused on multiple views of discrete spaces, that is, intense looking at a particular area, there are also single pictures of isolated areas within the garden that are not considered primary or that are at their off-season. Early spring is pictured in plates 53 and 54. In the former, winter hazel's blossoms dare the chill of the spring season's first days. In the latter, the bare winter branches offer a delicate tracery that screens our view toward the river. Groover photographed the Flower Garden at the end of winter, so her picture there (plate 55) offers an extreme contrast to standard views taken during warm weather. She placed her tripod outside of the Flower Garden, shooting from the side through the bare branches of the Japanese maple and the criss-crossing pattern of the wooden fence. The garden beyond lies empty and fallow. The day is overcast. The cold, bleak winter sky dominates.

The fourth picture in this group of miscellaneous and unusual views exemplifies in several ways Groover's approach to her experience at Wave Hill. In conversation, she dubbed plate 56 a "frenzied landscape." In it (as in plates 42 and 51), bare branches are read as a confusing entanglement. The center of the picture, instead of being a focal point of interest, is a void—a bizarre space created by the centrifugal movement of the surrounding plants.

Ironically, the photograph uses its seductive beauty to lead us into a space that provokes fear. Groover sends us mixed messages about the garden as a place. Admittedly, she demands that the space and place depicted in her picture convey feeling. She knows that, as the garden is beautiful, the pictures will and should be also. Groover's beauty is there, but it is not a pastoral or picturesque beauty. She is leery of pictorial ease or visual comfort. Any environment that lacks tension holds no interest for her. What she has done to ensure this tension is to seek places within the garden that appear quirky or confused, or to create through her camera compositions that place added emphasis on what is disturbing or chaotic, even in the built landscape.

When Groover, known for her extensive knowledge of the history of photography, is asked which pictures traditionally grouped in the category of landscape interest her, the answer is not surprising. First she asserts her lack of interest in heroic landscapes and the effort made by photographers to dupe viewers into believing they are literally standing before a landscape rather than looking at a picture. Then she mentions the Civil War–era photographers—George N. Barnard, Roger Fenton, and Mathew

B. Brady—who appeal to her because of their antiheroic approach; their landscapes are often bleak and empty rather than spiritually uplifting and full of interesting form. Groover's miscellaneous views of Wave Hill (plates 53–56) strive for a similar reversal of a romantic landscape aesthetic, be it by the hole in the center of a picture or the dominance of a flat sky. In pointing to what we may consider the less appealing aspects of an area, Groover elevates their visual plea.

The very first pictures that Groover took at Wave Hill undoubtedly will be associated with her work as a still-life photographer. These are the pictures taken in the cactus greenhouse. Here, on waist-high tables, old-world succulents and new-world cacti are displayed. The arrangement of the potted plants was a given. She could not move the elements around; however, her compositional approach was essentially the same as the one she employs in her studio. The space is shallow and, although the focus is on the plants in the foreground, she fully exploits as compositional devices the background of the greenhouse's metal framework and what is visible through the glazing.

Groover captures the collection-display purpose of the arrangement. The plants are laid out like objects in a museum study collection. They are not arranged with aesthetic intent as in the outdoor garden. It has been said that "Groover's crowded still lifes do what photographs can do better than any other medium (except, perhaps, words): make intoxicating lists."[23] This is surely the case, for these pictures objectively inventory the extent of the greenhouse display. At the same time, they subjectively present these plants as bizarre gifts of nature. Groover confuses our reading of their color, scale, arrangement, and relationship to their surroundings.

Although Groover approached the Wave Hill commission with eagerness, the beauty of her given subject made her cautious. Unable to compose artificially the edge-of-disaster feeling that characterizes her still lifes, she was determined to infiltrate the armchair ease of this landscape and subvert its somnolent effect. She strove for the tension and restlessness that make a subject interesting. Her vision does not allow us to be comfortable observers. It challenges us to rethink, refeel, and resee, so that our conception of what makes up the Wave Hill landscape must be reevaluated.

Groover has staunchly stood by the position that she is essentially a formalist, dedicated to creating eccentric compositions that seize our

visual interest. Photography is about looking. The photographer does not capture reality but self-consciously creates pictures that are visually captivating. She puts less stock in what is pictured than in how it is pictured. Fortunately for us, Groover found Wave Hill a rich vehicle for compositional exploration. Through her camera she penetrated this landscape, mining its beauty and visual complexity.

Stephen A. Scheer (born 1954)

came to the Wave Hill commission as a photographer with prior outdoor experience who was committed to working exclusively in color.[24] His early outdoor photographs chronicled the social, in particular suburban, landscape. In the late 1980s Scheer turned away from peopled environments and began photographing plant forms in the landscape, especially fruit trees. He saw the Wave Hill commission as an opportunity to experiment and develop more fully an approach to making color pictures that would communicate the experience of a particular place such as Wave Hill.

Scheer began taking pictures in his high-school camera club. Although he had it in mind

to pursue photography, he entered Bowdoin, a liberal arts college, in 1971, just before the age of the burgeoning studio art departments. He stayed on track, though, by majoring in art history. To supplement the limited studio curriculum, he took the year off in 1975 to study photography at the San Francisco Art Institute. He received his B.A. from Bowdoin College in 1976, took a two-year break, and then entered Yale University, graduating in 1980 with an M.F.A. in photography.

Scheer's earliest pictures were of landscapes, but this was not a genre he elected to pursue. At Bowdoin he focused on people, and at Yale, under the strong influence of Helen Levitt's work and the teaching of Nick Nixon and Todd Papageorge, he continued in this vein. It was at the San Francisco Art Institute that he began working in color. He worked both in black-and-white and in color until 1981, when he made the decision to work exclusively in color and to allow the chromatic aspects of picture making to play a significant role in his work.

Scheer divides his work after Yale into two periods: from 1980 to 1985 and from 1985–86 to the present. During the first period, his work fit loosely into the genres of social landscape or street photography. He would venture into suburban communities and attend festivals or special events, particularly during the summer, to catch middle-class citizens engaged in easygoing, leisure activities. Examples from a series taken in a residential Connecticut community called The Maples were included in *Aperture* under the title "America's Backyard." Young children were seen in small yards or on back porches with their red tricycles and assorted pets. Teenagers languished on the hoods of cars or cooled themselves under garden sprinklers. Scheer's statement introducing the *Aperture* portfolio indicates the tie he saw between the people and the place.

The residents have always liked to think of themselves as river people, and my intention was to document their style of life through color photography. Summer time seemed to bring out the most of what could be seen at The Maples. The people reunited with their natural surroundings, and their activity was refreshingly uninhibited and festive. I was particularly drawn to the way people adorned themselves and their surroundings, according to their age group and generation.[25]

A later group of pictures (1981–83) with similar intent was included in a photographic essay entitled "Summer States," in *New Color/New Work* by Sally Eauclaire. Again children sunbathe in modest yards or play games on residential streets. Bikes, garden hoses, beach chairs, towels, and barbecues are scattered about on patios and lawns.

In 1985 Scheer changed his subject matter and his technique. He turned from the social landscape to pure landscape and then to interior portraits with accompanying iconographically potent still-life arrangements. He quickly abandoned the landscapes to concentrate on the interior set-ups. He preferred working in a situation over which he had total control, including the assembling of the composition to be photographed. During this period he started using his own lighting, something he had learned about and had used for commercial jobs but had not considered for his own work. After the interior portraits came still-life groupings, frequently so large in scale that they were more appropriately labeled environments. Elements arranged for the sole purpose of picture making were scattered throughout the space of the room.

In 1987 Scheer returned to working outdoors, seeking rural settings, avoiding people altogether. He preferred trees, plants, flowers, and agricultural tools or garden implements, which he utilized in a manner similar to the arrangement of the iconographic elements in his interior portraits and environments. In keeping with his need to control the composition, Scheer continued to employ his own lighting, so these initial landscapes are characterized by a mix of natural and artificial light.

In these 1987 landscapes Scheer also introduced a major technical innovation, one that radically altered the look of his pictures and his method of picture making. He began working with the technique of double exposure, combining two views to produce a single picture. Each exposure was taken with a mix of light types. The result is a landscape picture more hyperreal than realistic. The Wave Hill pictures are the culmination of Scheer's experimentation with this process.

There are historical precedents for using more than one image to produce a final picture. Examples range from Gustave Le Gray's masking of negatives to provide his seascapes with appropriate skies to the most recent urban color photographs of Harry Callahan. Over the years, as technology and styles have changed, the specific technique and pictorial reasoning for using more than one image have evolved. Scheer connects with this history because of his desire to compose a synthetic picture.

The break between the social landscapes, portraits, and interior environments and the rural and garden landscapes is distinctive. The newer pictures look radically different and their content is unrelated. What Scheer learned from the street photography is significant, however, and it still guides him in his double-exposure work. Essential ingredients in the street pictures are suggested by Colin L. Westerbeck, Jr., and Martha Chahroudi in catalogues for exhibitions that included Scheer's street work. In his essay for *Color in the Street,* an exhibition held at the California Museum of Photography, University of California at Riverside, Westerbeck discusses the difference between street photography and photojournalism:

Photojournalists are people who are on the scene. They photograph what's there. Street photographers photograph what *isn't* there. They are interested in a reality that's symbolic rather than literal. They are trying to see what the imagination can invent out of the world, not what was actually going on at the moment they happened to take the picture. . . . This is not to say that street photography lies, but only that it creates fictions.[26]

Westerbeck's differentiation highlights the fictional and symbolic role of the street photographer, who extrapolates from the real world and creates for the viewer an image that is drawn from the street yet reaches beyond physical description for content. In making this distinction, Westerbeck illuminates a factor in Scheer's work that continues to affect his compositions after he has turned away from this genre. This intent clarifies the reasoning behind Scheer's highly idiosyncratic and technically complex approach to Wave Hill.

Martha Chahroudi, with credit to Nathan Lyons, points out in the catalogue for *Twelve Photographers Look at Us,* a 1987 exhibition at the Philadelphia Museum of Art, that social landscape photography exploits the relationships among depicted elements. Objects within an environment interact among themselves and with the context in which they are portrayed so as to alter themselves and one another. The result, in her words, is "suggestive of metaphoric meaning."[27] Scheer's Wave Hill pictures represent the culmination of a body of work that comes after the street pictures and is technically quite different yet which retains from the earlier pictures an emphasis on the

Stephen A. Scheer. Untitled (Positano). 1987.
From color original

photographer's imagination and inventiveness as well as the symbolic power of interrelationships and juxtapositions. Scheer may even have been timid in his use of the interrelationship among parts, holding his imagination in check during his pre-1985 work. Only more recently has he exploited these qualities to full advantage in the use of double exposure, the mix of natural and artificial light, and his move away from the suburban and into the garden landscape.

Scheer opted to pair his double-exposure and lighting techniques and allow them to dominate his working method for the considered reason that through them he could photograph *compositionally* in a way that was not possible with single-exposure, natural-light photography. Stating that he "thinks compositionally," as a photographer he is determined to exert the same control as a painter over the formal dynamics of his given subject.

Working outdoors with double exposure was strategically complex. Scheer's method involves no darkroom manipulation. Many people see the pictures and incorrectly assume that Scheer has superimposed two negatives; actually, he exposes one piece of film twice. He shoots in two locations in the garden so that one image is overlaid upon another in the camera. Scheer used two different cameras at Wave Hill: a 2¼ × 2¼" and a 4 × 5". The former produced square pictures and the latter horizontal or vertical ones. When using the 2¼" camera, Scheer would shoot both images on the same day. He would plan in advance as much as was possible, often using Polaroids to organize his composition. He would set up, take the first shot, move the camera and lights to the second location, set up, and then take the second. Thus, with the 2¼" camera the images were, for all practical purposes, simultaneous, with the overall composition pre-determined. With the 4 × 5" camera, Scheer used the option to expose the film one day and wait until the next to expose it a second time. The first image, therefore, was taken with some thought as to what the second might be but without a specific plan. Only when Scheer returned the next day did he finalize the location and set up his equipment for the second exposure. The final composition was not worked out in advance with Polaroids. This time-lapse approach was an idea that Scheer explored for the first time at Wave Hill. It moved him away from what he considers to be most photographers' working method, that is, to have a completed image in the mind's eye

Stephen A. Scheer. Untitled (Tuscany). 1987.
From color original

before shooting, which they then try to duplicate mechanically.

At Wave Hill Scheer was experimenting with a picture-making process that involved arriving at a completed picture through a series of steps by which the image was gradually built. Scheer took the first exposure knowing it to be an incomplete picture. In other words, he did not superimpose two pictures one upon another, but shot two unbalanced, partial images that when joined make a complete composition. The viewer should not be driven to disassemble the image into its original divided state, self-consciously breaking down and recombining the component parts. Rather, Scheer intends for the viewer to perceive a single, fluid image that portrays a unique composition synthesized from disparate elements that the photographer has used as compositional building blocks. The seam between the parts should be difficult to locate.

This image building is greatly enhanced by Scheer's mix of natural and artificial light. His use of electronic flash radically alters the composition. The artificial light, as much as the double exposure, removes Scheer's pictures from the realm of the natural and permits him to reinterpret light and shadow. Thus, he can use these natural properties in an unnatural, irrational manner, which leads to a reinterpretation of the space and the tonal and value changes, as well as an altered reading of the composition beyond that already created by the double exposure.

For those interested in the technical issues of photography, it is helpful to be aware of Scheer's methods. His technical dexterity and risk taking are impressive. His daily set-up was complex and time consuming. Each picture took a long working day. More pertinent and significant, however, is the end to which he puts this process and what he achieves through it in the Wave Hill pictures.

Like the other photographers, Scheer had never been to Wave Hill before he was invited to participate in this project. He first visited in May 1989. Once he accepted the invitation, he worked under a tighter schedule and over a shorter time period than the other photographers. Scheer's shortened work period, from May through October, rather than being a liability, actually turned into a fluke of circumstance that complemented his approach to the garden. The garden is at its peak from May to October. For those more interested in horticultural variety than in the broad structure of the garden, this is the time to visit. From early spring until late fall, every day at Wave Hill is one of major change. Only through daily walks and close scrutiny can one inventory the continuous evolution of the floral display.

Two primary characteristics of this evolving and constantly changing exhibition attracted Scheer and ultimately became guiding elements in his search for compositional elements. The first was brilliant color. Obviously the spring and summer flowers offered Scheer an extraordinary palette. The range and intensity of color available in the Flower Garden and the Wild Garden extend beyond any verbal description one may attempt. The second characteristic is the formal structure offered by the plants themselves. Because Wave Hill changes so rapidly during spring and summer, with plants coming into blossom, reaching their height, then falling back to be replaced by others, the structure of each bed, as well as the shape of trees and shrubs, changes quickly and radically. This constant flux, as opposed to a stable environment, held great appeal for Scheer.

Scheer would visit Wave Hill for three or four days in a row, wait a few days, and then return again for several more. Because it was his first season at Wave Hill, he had no knowledge of what to expect, especially in terms of the sequence of plantings. Every day was a surprise and what attracted him most frequently was not something he had seen before and become familiar with but something that was totally new—a flower in full bloom that only yesterday had been a closed bud. He eschewed overviews that took in the stable, larger forms that are the gardens' permanent skeleton and backbone. Instead, he photographed flowers against the context of a surrounding and supporting structure of plants, seeking out the gardens' most vibrant and fragile accents.

Scheer worked day by day, picture by picture, experimenting and learning from his own work as well as from the garden. He did not proceed in any serial fashion; he hopscotched from one spot to the next, guided by what was at its peak. His selections were made by the seductive appeal of one glorious visual delight over another.

Although there are no self-conscious groupings or subject-determined categories organizing Scheer's work, his pictures loosely fall into a few formal groupings. Within these groupings form and content are merged, as basic compositional similarities yield shared emotional results and symbolic emphasis.

Among the first group are many of Scheer's earliest pictures (plates 61–68). The scale of the space within these pictures is comfortable for the viewer. One can easily place oneself in the space of the compositions, or perhaps stand just outside looking in. Despite the double exposure, the space is easily read. It is not difficult to comprehend, nor is it unduly complex. The foreground, middle ground, and background are clear and the divisions between land and sky are realistic. Scheer relied on structural elements around which to build these compositions: the love seat in the Flower Garden, the columns of the pergola, a stone bench, a wall within the Dry Garden, or the trunk of the copper beech. Individual flowers or groups of blossoms of a single type are artificially lit so that they become prominent features in the picture. Examples of this effect can be seen in two isolated magnolia blossoms in plate 63, or in a shrub filled with lace-capped hydrangea in plate 64.

As a group, these first pictures are overtly romantic, perhaps reflecting Scheer's initial response to Wave Hill as a place of sensuous beauty and easy grace, where the aroma and aura of spring flowers are mesmerizing. This romanticism is epitomized in plate 61. The roses dominating the picture are captured just a moment after their peak, and this sets the tone for the entire composition. The intimate love seat around which the roses climb offers a promise of romance, although the petals scattered on the garden floor connote defeat. All this is set against a backdrop of evergreens and a moody sky suggesting another place and time. Even as these elements combine to intimate melancholy, the intense light on the roses in the right middle ground snaps us out of this mood and draws us back into the clear sunlight of the present day.

The second group employs close-up views of plant fragments (plates 69–71). These compositions bear no relationship to the scale or order of so-called real space. Spatial unreality and intense artificial light on the plants dominate. The actual size of individual plants is unknown for they are not set within knowable space. The plants are depicted without knowledge of their original context. In plate 69 a shiny magnolia branch comes from an unknown source to bisect the picture diagonally. Hibiscus, daylilies, and spruce intermix in plate 71. The combinations are, from a horticultural standpoint, absurd. We know plants do not grow this way and that no gardener would purposefully plant in these combinations.

The scale of garden plants is supposed to be comfortable and nonthreatening. The light should be soothing, never harsh or glaring. Plants should be arranged in pleasing combinations that never jar the eye. Growth patterns are understood and held in check. Scheer has created pictures that violate these laws of garden design and garden-viewing enjoyment. His compositions are based on awkward arrangements, disconcerting lighting, and threatening scale. We are unsettled in response. Through these pictures our expectations are challenged and the symbolic and expressive vocabulary of garden plants enlarged.

Scheer's remaining nine pictures emphasize this greater risk taking in terms of composition building. They fall easily into two groups. Plates 72–74 are Scheer's triumphal compositions. In each he lifts floral groupings from different sections of the garden and rearranges them into compositions that are basically triangular, hierarchical configurations. This formal arrangement has religious connotations, recalling Christian iconography. In plate 72 a bunch of yellow flowers overlays a pine and an elm. This gigan-

tic bouquet floats upward in a cloud-filled summer sky, a resurrection composition with a surreal twist.

Water lilies crown the composition in plate 73. They are diminutive and, in terms of space and scale, minor in the overall picture. They should be insignificant compared to the plant abundance beneath them. This, however, is not the case; these tiny plants serve as the compositional apex, giving order to what otherwise would be a confusing jumble. Scheer takes great liberty in crowning a triangular composition with white lilies, the traditional symbol of purity. In plate 74 there is again religious implication, this time of the transfiguration, as one element is transposed into another. Because of the pool, the grasses that cascade into it read as flowing water, a symbol of cleansing and rejuvenation. A stone path miraculously extends itself across the surface of the pond.

In these three pictures, the rules of gravity do not apply and boundaries between objects do not exist. There is no differentiation between air and matter or liquids and solids. These are pre-Renaissance compositions in which the space is filled with detail yet the form is dematerialized. Spirit and symbol rule over matter.

In plates 75–80 Scheer has reintroduced gravity and a greater sense of the materiality of form. He has widened the expanse of his vision and in this more open space continues to explore adventurous formal juxtapositions. These pictures are more lyrical and carefree, even though the mix of artificial and natural light continues to provide a grand theatricality and a slightly disturbing edge. One of Scheer's last pictures (plate 78), taken during the fall, is an excellent example of his lyricism. The central element is a silver maple set against and in scale with a dramatic landscape and sky. The second exposure is of another tree, of increased scale, with red leaves and bright red berries. The result is a joyous composition that communicates the splendor of the fall season as is possible only in the rambling hillsides and river valleys of the American Northeast.

All of Scheer's pictures are characterized by the overlaying of images. Because of this sandwiching, some forms are clear, bright, and completely articulated; others are murky, seen through a haze or screen and thus only partially readable. They appear in the distance, just beyond our visual grasp. Sometimes the outline of a form will be clear and perfectly intelligible. We read a maple tree as a maple tree, but then its existence will be voided when its trunk is transformed into an evergreen. From its branches fall not maple leaves but the fruits of the trifoliate orange. We may be certain of the existence and identification of a particular plant, like the mullein in plate 60; its strong stalk and yellow flowers are unmistakable. But then our eye moves downward and its base transforms itself into a hosta.

Strangely, none of this leads to mental fatigue or emotional messiness. There is a familiarity to these pictures that belies the fact that they are Scheer's own compositions and not those of a Wave Hill gardener. This is particularly true for garden lovers who allow themselves to be overtaken by the garden's impact, who relinquish themselves to the experiential nature of the garden visit and who later relish the remembered images of a place. For these people, Scheer's pictures are recognized as photographs about the experience itself. Remembered experience originates, not from a series of isolated images, but through a combination of moments and visions that merge in the memory and the mind's eye. Our brain stores information with different degrees of clarity. Our recall is not consistent, nor is it sequential. In memory, images overlap, combine and recombine as we try to recall what being in a place felt and looked like.

The landscape designer uses plants to build a garden. Scheer has photographed flowering plants and composed unique pictures in order to communicate his impression and memory of a landscape. His dramatic reorganizations are tied to his daily experience at Wave Hill. His pictures relate the nature of that experience and the myriad horticultural events that contributed to its making. Scheer was a garden visitor who allowed himself to be overwhelmed by the abundance and life-giving properties of the Wave Hill gardens. He believed that straight, descriptive pictures would do a disservice to this plethora. Thus, he composed his own pictures, which theatrically dramatize the colorful and complex world of the Wave Hill garden.

Jean E. Feinberg

NOTES

1. John Szarkowski, *American Landscapes* (New York: The Museum of Modern Art, 1981), 5.

2. Weston J Naef and James N. Wood, *Era of Exploration: The Rise of Landscape Photography in the American West, 1860–1885* (Boston: New York Graphic Society, 1975), 12, 16.

3. *The Art of Photography 1839–1989* (London: The Royal Academy of Arts, and Houston: Museum of Fine Arts, 1989). Examples of garden pictures in this catalogue include the following: William Henry Fox Talbot's *A Bush of Hydrangea in Flower*, mid-1840s; Louis-Rémy Robert's *Versailles, Fountain of the Pyramid of Girardon*, 1853; Gustave Le Gray's *Beech Tree in the Forest of Fontainebleau*, before 1858; Roger Fenton's *The Long Walk* and *View in the Slopes, Windsor*, 1860; Felice A. Beato's *Tycoons' Halting Place on the Tocaido Hasa*, 1868; Robert MacPherson's *Grotto at Tivoli*, c. 1860; Peter Henry Emerson's *A Snow Garden*, 1895; Frederick H. Evans's *Untitled (Chateau Garden)*, c. 1906–9; Edward Steichen's *Trees, Long Island*, 1905; Clarence H. White's *The Orchard*, 1902; Alfred Stieglitz's *Grapes and Vines*, 1933; László Moholy-Nagy's *Untitled (view into courtyard garden from Berlin Radio Tower)*, 1928; Eugène Atget's *Parc de Sceaux*, 1921; Diane Arbus's *A Family on Their Lawn One Sunday in Westchester, New York*, 1969; Joel Sternfeld's *Buckingham, Pennsylvania, August 1978*; Josef Sudek's *My Garden with the Wash Hanging*, 1965; William Eggleston's *Tallahatchie County, Mississippi*, 1971; Robert Adam's *Untitled (from 'Denver' series)*, 1973; and Ian

Macdonald's *Mandy Jemmerson and Paula Woods Drawing Hedgerows, Secondary School, Cleveland,* 1983.

4. John Szarkowski and James Alinder, *Ansel Adams: Classic Images* (Boston: Little, Brown and Company), 6.

5. John Szarkowski and Maria Morris Hambourg, *The Work of Atget,* 4 vols. (New York: The Museum of Modern Art, 1983), 1:177, 190.

6. Ibid., 1:25, 26.

7. Tim Davis, "Photography and Landscape Studies," *Landscape Journal* (Spring 1989): 5, 8, 10.

8. All biographical information on Conner, Groover, Trager, and Scheer was obtained through a series of conversations between the photographers and the author.

9. For reproduction purposes, Conner makes silver prints. The duotones in this volume were made from silver prints, with the platinum prints available for comparison. The goal was to duplicate as much of a platinum look as the duotone process could provide.

10. Conner's original impetus for traveling particularly to Guilin, China, was its renowned forests, the subject of painters and poets for two thousand years.

11. John Szarkowski, *The Photographer's Eye* (New York: The Museum of Modern Art, 1966), unpaginated.

12. Ibid.

13. Philip Trager, *Photographs of Architecture* (Middletown, Conn.: Wesleyan University Press, 1977).

14. Philip Trager, *Philip Trager: New York* (Middletown, Conn.: Wesleyan University Press, 1980).

15. After Trager accepted the Wave Hill commission, he requested using Wave Hill as a setting for his dance pictures. He then photographed several dance companies on the grounds of Wave Hill during the summers of 1988 and 1989.

16. Richard Pare, *Photography and Architecture 1839–1939* (Montreal: Canadian Centre for Architecture, 1982), 17.

17. For an explanation of this site-specific installation, titled *WAVE HILL GREEN,* see Jean E. Feinberg, *Perceiving the Garden: Robert Irwin at Wave Hill* (Wave Hill, 1987).

18. Szarkowski and Hambourg, *The Work of Atget,* 1:163.

19. In *The Work of Atget,* 4:26, Szarkowski has stated, "To ask which contemporary photographers have been influenced by Atget is no more fruitful than to ask which contemporary painters have been influenced by Matisse or Picasso or Mondrian. His work, like theirs, has long been a systematic part of the tradition; it and Atget are no longer wholly separable." Thus it cannot be overemphasized how strong Atget is, as a figure to emulate and pay tribute to, or as a figure to consciously work against, in the minds of all contemporary photographers as they approach parks, gardens, or the cultivated countryside. While this influence is being noted particularly for Trager's lawn pictures, it holds true equally for many of Conner's pictures. Groover, on the other hand, determinedly used her knowledge of Atget to avoid obvious homage to his garden pictures.

20. Ibid., 1:168.

21. These were pictures taken in Washington, D.C., and commissioned by the Corcoran Gallery as part of the Bicentennial Celebration.

22. Susan Kismaric, *Jan Groover* (New York: The Museum of Modern Art, 1987), unpaginated.

23. Ben Lifson, "Jan Groover's Embrace," *Aperture* 85 (1981): 36.

24. Philip Trager and Jan Groover both began photographing in color and black-and-white. Only after developing preliminary pictures did Trager commit to black-and-white and Groover to color.

25. Stephen A. Scheer, "America's Backyard," *Aperture* 91 (1983): 40–47.

26. Colin L. Westerbeck, Jr., "Some Notes on the Exhibition," *California Museum of Photography Bulletin,* vol. 1, no. 5: 14.

27. Martha Chahroudi, "Twelve Photographers Look at US," *Philadelphia Museum of Art Bulletin,* vol. 83, nos. 354, 355 (Spring 1987): 3.

The
Photographs

Lois Conner

PLATE ONE

PLATE TWO

PLATE THREE

PLATE FOUR

PLATE FIVE

PLATE SIX

PLATE SEVEN

PLATE EIGHT

PLATE NINE

PLATE TEN

PLATE ELEVEN

PLATE TWELVE

PLATE THIRTEEN

PLATE FOURTEEN

PLATE FIFTEEN

PLATE SIXTEEN

PLATE SEVENTEEN

PLATE EIGHTEEN

PLATE NINETEEN

PLATE TWENTY

Philip Trager

PLATE TWENTY-ONE

PLATE TWENTY-TWO

PLATE TWENTY-THREE

PLATE TWENTY-FOUR

PLATE TWENTY-FIVE

PLATE TWENTY-SIX

PLATE TWENTY-SEVEN

PLATE TWENTY-EIGHT

PLATE TWENTY-NINE

PLATE THIRTY

PLATE THIRTY-ONE

PLATE THIRTY-TWO

PLATE THIRTY-THREE

PLATE THIRTY-FOUR

PLATE THIRTY-FIVE

PLATE THIRTY-SIX

PLATE THIRTY-SEVEN

PLATE THIRTY-EIGHT

PLATE THIRTY-NINE

PLATE FORTY

Jan Groover

PLATE FORTY-ONE

PLATE FORTY-TWO

PLATE FORTY-THREE

PLATE FORTY-FOUR

PLATE FORTY-FIVE

PLATE FORTY-SIX

PLATE FORTY-SEVEN

PLATE FORTY-EIGHT

PLATE FORTY-NINE

PLATE FIFTY

PLATE FIFTY-ONE

PLATE FIFTY-TWO

PLATE FIFTY-THREE

PLATE FIFTY-FOUR

PLATE FIFTY-FIVE

PLATE FIFTY-SIX

PLATE FIFTY-SEVEN

PLATE FIFTY-EIGHT

PLATE FIFTY-NINE

PLATE SIXTY

Stephen A. Scheer

PLATE SIXTY-ONE

PLATE SIXTY-TWO

PLATE SIXTY-THREE

PLATE SIXTY-FOUR

PLATE SIXTY-FIVE

PLATE SIXTY-SIX

PLATE SIXTY-SEVEN

PLATE SIXTY-EIGHT

PLATE SIXTY-NINE

PLATE SEVENTY

PLATE SEVENTY-ONE

PLATE SEVENTY-TWO

PLATE SEVENTY-THREE

PLATE SEVENTY-FOUR

PLATE SEVENTY-FIVE

PLATE SEVENTY-SIX

PLATE SEVENTY-SEVEN

PLATE SEVENTY-EIGHT

PLATE SEVENTY-NINE

PLATE EIGHTY

Wave Hill: History of a Place

Wave Hill stretches along the west-facing slope above the Hudson River, opposite the Palisades, in a looping series of buildings, gardens, pathways, and lawns constructed on and between terraces. The main terrace, large enough to appear on Federal topographic maps as part of the contour of the hillside, forms the central lawn which is supported by a retaining wall sixty yards long and ten yards high. In the center of the wall, silhouetted against the Palisades and the sky, is a pergola, from which the river and the Palisades afford an unparalleled natural vista that few could imagine existing within New York City. A mile across the river, the Palisades rise two hundred feet higher than the pergola and lawn, creating a natural trick of perspective that sometimes leads to the illusion that the land forms are in motion. From this vantage point one not only discovers the Hudson's great gorge but can imagine witnessing its creation.

The ridge from which one views this natural wonder is a deliberate landscape. With practice and the proper questions, elements of Wave Hill can be read as artifacts. A retaining wall and terraced garden and a stone wall through the woods are like scratches on the surface of scrimshaw, or the patterns in a fragment of Native American Woodland pottery. An object of bronze, stone, or clay has the capacity to transport us across time, to connect us to the maker of the object, to the way of living that engendered it. Land is merely a different sort of artifact. Its surface is animate and records its history differently. Today's woodland was once a colonial pasture. A plant in the garden may be a specimen of an old variety, cloned by gardeners for six hundred years. The changes in the land are part of the record. Time and change are elements of "a sense of place." Once we have lived on a place and tended it, we are part of its past, and we are connected to others by imagining how they responded to the land and changed it.

This place on the land, Wave Hill, is twenty-eight acres of rocks and soil and living biomass arranged in terraces on the slope above the river. The terraces continue down the slope, below the pergola, below lawns and houses and into the woods, where farm terraces slump above dry, crumbling stone walls. Below the last of these old walls, at the edge of a natural terrace, is a big, double-trunked tupelo, or black-gum tree, which dominates this place in the woods. To approach it is to enter a room, a stage set. Light darkens from yellow to deep green. The air becomes damp and sweeter. Sounds grow softer. Ferns and mayapple grow in the thick leaf litter beneath this tree. Ecologists call this place a micro-environment. Created by years of shade, it is a patch of the old primary forest growing within the young woods.

The tupelo seeded in naturally. Its seeds are borne in small blue, plumlike fruit and probably transported by birds. This tree began its life a century ago as a woody weed at the edge of a garden, and it grew here as a sapling while this meadow was mowed once each year. It was cut at least once along with the meadow grass into which it had seeded. It renewed itself the next year with two sprouts from its roots. Then someone decided not to cut the tree, perhaps because tupelo have fine long-lasting fall foliage and they make good shade. Whatever the reason, the tree was allowed to grow, first on the eastern edge of a cultivated field and later, when farming ceased, alone in an open meadow.

Tupelo is a species of the southern Piedmont forest. Here, in the lower Hudson Valley, the New England hardwood forest and the southern forest met and mixed. They produced the primary forest that Henry Hudson found in 1609, a patchwork of open Indian planting fields along the river and awesome, parklike woodlands of giant trees above both shores—the Native American's hunting orchards, which the Europeans called wilderness. Carolina wrens nested with black-capped chickadees. The flora and fauna of this region were as rich and varied as in any temperate forest in the New World. Tupelo and sassafras grew next to sugar maples, basswood, and birch. Journals of the early Europeans describe the approach to New Amsterdam and the harbor at the mouth of the North River as filled with the sweet airs of this flora.

The double trunks of the tree testify that this is a sprout species, as are most of the species of the hardwood forests of eastern North America. These are forests that have developed with humankind by a process of selection favoring those hardwood species best able to survive the burning practices of the Native Americans and, later, the cattle grazing of farmers.

This land had once been part of the Philipse Grant that ran along the Hudson from the Bronx into Westchester County.[1] Philipse was a Tory, and his land was seized by the government and sold off in parcels by the Commissioners of Forfeiture. In 1779 this parcel was purchased by a farmer named George Hadley.

Deforestation in the regions around northeastern cities had become commonplace. The lumber required to build and heat the city, and then to warm two wintering armies, had come from the Bronx and the accessible eastern shore of the Hudson. Thus, the land Hadley bought had been cleared. The flat, tillable terrace above the river and the formerly wooded slope were dotted with stumps and littered with slash from the clear cutting that had deforested the region by the end of the Revolution.

Hadley might have been among the first farmers to plant black locust, a species brought north from the southern mountains as a fast-growing cash crop that could be sold for fence posts. Also, young locust trees are covered with thorns and can coexist in pastures with grazing cattle. By the time George Hadley sold the land twenty years later, the locusts had begun to naturalize.

In the 1790s two farmers owned the land. William Ackerman owned the north half of the property and John Westervelt the south. Their property lines are marked by the remains of a stone wall in the woods and a service road behind the greenhouse.

By the mid-nineteenth century, agriculture had moved north and west of the city. Ackerman, who worked the land for almost fifty years, had died. Farming often ends with the passing of a generation, and, when the William Morrises bought the property in 1836 from Ackerman's heirs, the land was slowly being overtaken by brush and thorny young black locust trees.

William Lewis Morris and his wife, Mary Elizabeth Babcock, were members of old New York families. It is not known why they decided to buy this land. Perhaps they took the advice of Samuel Thompson, a successful builder-developer who was investing heavily in Yonkers real estate and who had bought the land south of Wave Hill in 1835. Plans were underway for the rail line along the river's eastern shore, which would bring this land within easy reach of the city and enhance its value. In 1836 the Morrises purchased fifteen acres of river frontage and slope side and in 1843 built their "Yonkers farm."

They sited the house on the prow of a promontory above the river and named the property "Wave Hill." Its northern boundary was a gully, probably containing a seasonal intermittent brook, or freshet, and an old wagon road that ran over the top of the ridge straight down the slope to a natural landing at a marsh. The southern boundary of the property was the edge of a larger cleft in the slope carved by Ice Age glaciers near the point where soft Inwood marble, the bedrock of the valley, meets Fordham gneiss, the bedrock of the promontory.

From the east the house was reached by the wagon road. Descending the gully next to the freshet and sheltered by small trees on either side, one could see the Palisades straight ahead but would not see the house until the road veered to the left at the entrance. Here the traveler would discover a two-story stone structure jutting up on a point of land, standing alone toward the bottom of a cleared, open slope against the mile-wide river and the rim of the Palisades. A few old trees remained on the hillside. The trees in the field to the west of the house were growing in farmland, and at least three are still there today: a black cherry, a giant American elm, and a large old sugar maple. Norway and sycamore maple, honeysuckle, and porcelainberry vine had not yet appeared on the hillside, which would have had the look and the color of southern New England farmland.

From the boat landing, which the Morrises shared with Samuel Thompson, the house was reached by an improved carriage road, which probably followed the tracks of the log sleds of the woodcutters who had cleared the land eighty years earlier. The approach to the house on this road afforded a new vista on each leg of the trip. From the dock the road ran north along the river on the natural terrace until it turned sharply southeast and began a series of shallow inclines up the slope. At first the river dropped from sight and the roof of the house could be glimpsed above the edge of the promontory and against the sky. On the last leg of the trip, heading south, the river stretched out ahead. One could almost see Manhattan. The house was on the left, and on the right the road just traveled curled up from the river. Today there are trees in the parkland that had been cultivated fields before farmer Ackerman died, and the drama of the view from the carriage road can be seen in the light reflected through the trees, a shining glimpse of how it must have appeared 150 years ago.

Panorama of the Hudson, a series of diagrammatic illustrations of the shores of the Hudson as seen from the river, published in 1845, includes the first known image of Wave Hill. The

Riverdale ridge appears as a patchwork of pasture land and brushy second growth. Without pattern, the profile of the ridge is punctuated by single tall trees, often white pines, perhaps remnants of the earlier forest. The panoramas of other sections of the shore differentiate cultivated land from pasture; no cultivated land is shown on the diagram. The perspective is contrived to reveal a larger area of the ridge and to locate more homes of the rich. The Morris house appears near the bottom, close to the river, where the name "Morris" floats with the names of neighbors.

Mary Morris died at Wave Hill in 1851 and William moved back to Manhattan, where he died in 1864. In 1865 their heirs permitted a connecting carriage road to be cut through the center of the property in order to provide access for new homes and an east-west route along the ridge to the new Riverdale railroad station. This road was the first major change in the shape of the land since the house was built, slicing through the field that had swept down from the top of the ridge. The house now stood in a smaller, yardlike space. It was less isolated, no longer alone at the bottom of a long pasture, less of an outpost on the edge of nature.

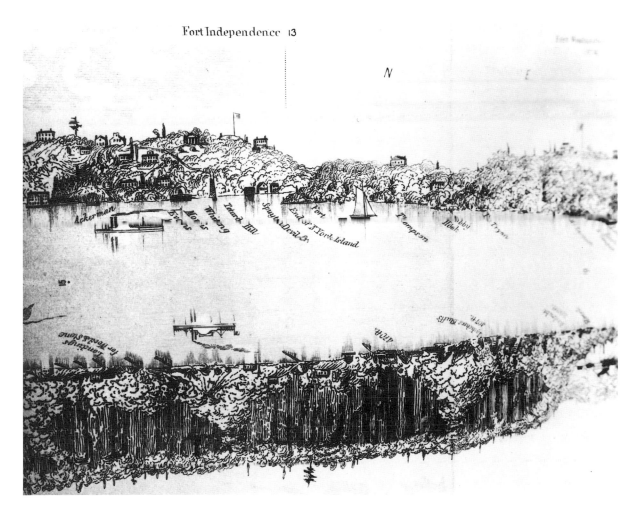

View of Riverdale from William Wades, *Panorama of the Hudson.* 1845. Photograph Wave Hill Archives

The Hudson River Railroad was chartered in 1847. The first track was completed to Yonkers in 1849, and the Riverdale Station had become a regular post-office stop by 1864. The first tracks, built with the least possible investment in earth moving, hugged the shore. The effect was picturesque, and the scene was often included in the romantic paintings of the Hudson Valley, from which other signs of encroaching civilization were omitted. Before the railroad, Riverdale had been isolated from New York City. It had been reachable by boat, a trip that the tides and currents made undependable, or by a wagon road up the steep escarpment of the Riverdale ridge from the Inwood marble valley (through which Broadway now runs). The railroad, which would one day transform the eastern shore of the river, made it possible to create an idyllic suburban community on this otherwise isolated ridge.

The Morris family had owned the land for thirty years. In this time the landscape matured, gradually changing from farmland to a country suburban neighborhood in a process similar to the changes that would occur a century later in New York City's outer ring of Fairfield, Suffolk, Westchester, and Rockland counties. In 1866, the year after the new road was put in, Wave Hill was purchased by William Henry Appleton, partner with his father in the publishing enterprise of D. Appleton and Company. He modernized the house, changing it from a simple, two-story Greek-revival farmhouse into a three-story Victorian villa with a mansard roof. The transformation took more than two years to complete. The entry was shifted to the east side of the house, facing the new front lawn. Appleton changed the name Wave Hill to Holbrook Hall, replacing the name of a place on the land with the name of a building. On the front lawn he planted copper beeches and European lindens, which are there today, part of the "design" of the area in front of the house. Some of the few contemporary photographs of the area show stone and wooden houses along unpaved streets, dwarfed by large trees—among them American chestnuts and American elms—arching toward the sky.

In the summers of 1870 and 1871 the Appletons rented Holbrook Hall to the Theodore Roosevelt family, which included twelve-year-old Theodore, Jr. Teddy's diary describes exploring the neighborhood, playing in the brook above Henry Foster Spaulding's riverside villa, climbing trees, building huts in the woods, searching for birds' nests, riding a pony, and swimming with friends. According to his sister, these were the summers in which Teddy's interest in natural history first manifested itself.

The ridge must have held the same fascination for Teddy Roosevelt as it holds for children today. To walk down a familiar, tree-lined street and discover the river and the cliffs where more of the neighborhood had been expected is—even for an adult—like discovering the Grand Canyon just beyond the edge of the backyard. The geography of the ridge affords the imagination easy access to another, awesome world. For Teddy, going through farm fields, down at the bottom of the ridge and out from under the line of trees that grew on the slope just above the river's shore, was a short trip to a place that felt like the edge of the world. Even today, despite the detritus of the railroad, the wind from across the water and the massive wall of the Palisades against the sky from horizon to horizon are utterly convincing—you have entered another world, discovered a new continent, and are standing opposite the wall that is the perimeter of the earth.

In his last years there, Appleton added a dining wing to the house, which now loomed considerably larger in front of the Palisades. He died at Holbrook Hall in 1899. From October 1899 to June 1903, the place was rented to his friend and client Samuel Langhorne Clemens, whose stay at Holbrook Hall marked the end of an era in the history of this landscape. While it lasted Clemens enjoyed it:

And how the stormy winds do blow, as the sailor ballad says. I believe we have the noblest roaring blasts here I have ever known on land; they sing their hoarse song through the big tree-tops with a splendid energy that thrills me and stirs me and uplifts me and makes me want to live always.[2]

His daughter remembered:

There was one chestnut tree so large that a platform had been built in its branches, holding table and chairs for a tea party. A wooden staircase led up to the branches. Father sometimes sat in this tree parlor with a fragrant corn-cob pipe. He also made notes there for articles and speeches.[3]

Chestnut leaves are leathery and oaklike, and these big trees were as good as oaks at singing hoarse songs in the wind. Naturally occurring chestnuts belonged with the elm, sugar maple, and black cherry; they were there in the farm fields where the Morrises had constructed their "Yonker's farm." Some of these trees remain today, but not the chestnuts. Even as Clemens sat in his chestnut "tree parlor," the tree and those around it were dying of blight.

Between 1895 and 1920 there were more changes to the shape of the land in the valley than at any time since the great Ice Age. The view of the Palisades from the pergola is so natural, vast, and impressive that it is difficult to believe that this land form is not solely the consequence of volcanism and glacial activity. It appears to be a scene only God could have made.

In spite of the awe the river inspires, its valley is not the one Henry Hudson saw in 1609 nor the one in which Teddy Roosevelt played. The colors of the rocks and foliage, the shapes of the shorelines and cliffs are different. Rock quarries and the railroad made the difference.

The slope at the base of the Palisades had been a source of ballast since the early seventeenth century, when trading ships sailed into the Hudson, and of building stone since the first settlers moved onto the western shore. Large-scale quarrying of the Palisades began around 1895, after the invention of dynamite made it possible and a market was created for traprock as bedding for city streets and railroad tracks. Using its powers of condemnation, the New York City Department of Street Improvement was by 1895 already well along in its mission to create a modern city on the sites of old farms in northern Manhattan. The newly annexed Bronx was next: In 1895 the Department announced a "scientific and uniform" street pattern that would follow the construction of the rapid rail systems north into the farmlands of the Bronx, carving it into valuable city lots. Great fortunes were made by speculators who preceded the new streets north, and smaller fortunes were made by the quarry owners who supplied the bedding for this massive urban development project.

The railroad system was expanding also. A new Harlem Line up the Saw Mill River Valley and another, through the Ramapo Fault and north along the preglacial course of the river, spurred the expansion of the Hudson River Line. The more successful and competitive the railroads became, the more earth they were capable of moving and the more traprock they consumed as ballast for their tracks.

The quarry industry on the western shore of the Hudson exploded. From south of Fort

View of Holbrook Hall from the southwest. 1903.
Photograph Wave Hill Archives

Lee to Hook Mountain, the face of the cliffs and its rim were stripped of trees. The same qualities of cleavage and fracturing that had made the cliffs susceptible to glacial ice were exploited by the quarriers. An explosive charge at the base of the cliffs resulted in an avalanche of almost market-ready stone. One quarry staged public events whenever it destroyed distinctive and memorable pinnacles. In places, the entire face of the cliff was obscured by two-hundred-foot-high heaps of broken stone. More than a hundred quarries extracted tens of millions of tons of traprock. Barges tied up to multistory, smoke-belching, whistling stone crushers that finished the job the blasting had begun. In the process, the face of the cliffs was made smooth and moved westward. The cliffs were diminishing and in places had disappeared altogether.

The public outcry to save the Palisades from obliteration grew on both sides of the river. Numerous plans to save the cliffs, including one to make them a military reservation, failed to gain legislative support, but finally the movement prevailed in 1900, when the Palisades Park Commission was established.

The governors of New York and New Jersey each named five members to the new Commission. George W. Perkins, appointed by New York governor Theodore Roosevelt, was elected its first chairman. Perkins lived in Riverdale, and when he purchased Holbrook Hall from the Appleton family in 1903 he may have desired a better view of the progress his work was making on the opposite shore. By the time he moved into Holbrook Hall, much of the Palisades had already been saved. As chairman of the Commission, Perkins had raised private contributions to buy the quarries faster than the processes of legislative appropriations or public condemnation would have permitted. In fact, in the Commission's first seven years, it acquired more than 140 parcels of the Palisades and created the nucleus of the future park.

Perkins was a successful businessman, associated with both the Morgan Bank and the New York Life Insurance Company. At the same time he worked for the public good to save the Palisades, he used his personal wealth to create a private compound on the eastern slope above the river, accumulating some eighty acres, at a cost of half a million dollars. His first purchase had been the Spaulding estate, which had its own beach, landing, and water garden. The second was a house at the south end of the property, which became Perkins's home. Holbrook Hall was one of his last purchases, the third property to be consolidated into the center of his estate.

The Spaulding estate contains one of many large old houses along the Hudson's eastern shore that were built atop great lawns that swept down to the river's edge. The railroad's gradual expansion isolated these houses from the river and, as the widening track beds slowly ate away their greenswards, altered the scale of their sites, so that today these houses sit above the tracks like amputees. In its final expansion in 1909, the railroad buried the water garden, pools, and pathways Spaulding had built on the shore, at the bottom of a wide fieldstone stairway. The remains of these gardens are found in the woods as giant specimens of ornamental Japanese cut-leaf maples, an acre of shaded, blossomless daylilies, and the partially buried stone walkways that circled blue perennial beds.

Unlike the blasting of the Palisades, the destruction of the eastern shore of the Hudson happened a little at a time. But by 1909, when it was completed, the railroad had made the river's edge into a place of factories and sidings, docks and worker housing. Life and land values along the river had been drastically altered. The rich moved up the slope away from the river. If they did not move their houses, they moved the centers of their outdoor life, building gardens and greenhouses, tennis courts and swimming pools.

Andrew Jackson Downing provided the philosophy of this movement with essays about the value of long, distant views. Even perceptions about public health contributed to the migration: living near the water was thought to be dangerous. Ornamental ponds in Central Park and throughout New York City were drained for reasons of public health. A distant view of the river was deemed fashionable and healthful and was certainly more pleasant than looking too closely at what was happening to the valley below.

Although Perkins's accumulation of land had kept the speculators at bay, New York City's Department of Street Improvement kept coming. Perkins's move up the slope involved escaping the railroad, blocking the road builders, and creating a unified hillside estate out of three previously separate properties. To accomplish these objectives was a major construction project, so large it changed the contours of the ridge.

View of the east façade, Holbrook Hall. 1912–14. Photograph Wave Hill Archives

View of the upper and lower terraces created by the recreation building. 1911–12. Photograph Wave Hill Archives

The project consisted of the construction of the retaining wall that supports the central lawn. Below this wall a two-story structure, built partially underground and into the side of the slope, served as a family recreation center (it is now the Archaeology and Ecology Building). Next to a swimming pool, it housed a bowling alley, rifle range, squash court, pool cabana, play room, servants' quarters, and workshop. The Bronx Building Department attempted to prevent the construction of the recreation center, but Perkins appealed to the City Corporation Counsel, who affirmed that as long as private property had yet to be condemned for public access, the owner was free to proceed as he saw fit. As a further deterrent to the Department of Street Improvement, a coachman's lodge and a gardener's cottage were moved, combined into a single house, and placed in the path of a proposed street.

The terraced lawn above the retaining wall was created using the rock and earth removed from the excavation for the new building, the roof of which became a terrace. The removal of the coachman's lodge made space for a tennis court and a more expansive central lawn in front of the greenhouses and rose garden. The yard and foundation of the gardener's cottage, which had stood in the upper corner of the Holbrook Hall property, became the garden at the height of land in the middle of the Perkins estate. A water-lily pond was added north of this garden. A shaded wildflower garden was built in the wooded area at the south end of the property on the ancient bank of the river.

The center of this new estate was the pergola at the top of the giant retaining wall. The roof terrace below the pergola, planted in a sea of tulips, screened the railroad from view and served as a proscenium for the drama of nature being reconstructed on the opposite shore. The pergola was ideally situated to extol the virtues of the Palisades Park and to raise money for it. Perkins must have used this spot to describe the Park's expanding public use and the need to improve the plantings along its shoreline drive, the removal of the last debris of the quarries, and the construction of swimming, camping, and boating areas. Between 1909 and 1917 he raised millions of dollars to improve the amenities of the Park, to staff it with grounds keepers and lifeguards, and to provide access via ferries from Manhattan. It had become one of America's most popular, most visited public parks.

Between the years 1895 and 1920 there was another important and powerful change in the landscape of this valley and of the eastern United States. It was biological in origin, a silent, ominous background event. It was the region's first lesson that nature does not always renew itself, nor can it be compelled to do so. These were the years the American chestnut vanished from the land. These giants with their horizontally spreading branches, the singers of hoarse songs, these remnant jewels of the wilderness forest succumbed to a blight. It is more difficult to perceive changes in the land that is lived on every day than it is to return to a place one has known well and loved—a childhood home, a marsh in which one has hunted frogs—and to find it almost unrecognizable. When Theodore Roosevelt returned to the shores of this river to help save the Palisades from the destruction of the quarries, the land was not as he had experienced it in his youth. It must have felt naked and threatened, because the chestnuts were dying.

George Perkins died on June 18, 1920, at age fifty-eight. Six years later his house was damaged by a thunderstorm, which brought lightning, a fire on the roof, and several days of torrential rain. Mrs. Perkins replaced it with a

smaller building. In 1928 a new wing—a Gothic two-story museum—was added to the main house. The museum wing, built to display the armor collection of Bashford Dean, a tenant in the house, continued the lateral expansion of the building that had begun with Appleton's dining wing. In 1930, the Perkinses' daughter, Mrs. Edward Freeman, removed all Victorian features, restoring the classical lines of the original house and adding a service wing on the south to balance the Armor Hall on the north. The changes completed the architectural wall between the front of the house and the river. The extended house created two spaces at the edge of the promontory, the enclosed front yard and the open expanse of the west lawn.

Mr. and Mrs. Freeman changed the name "Holbrook Hall" back to "Wave Hill." They also added to the front lawn a row of sweet gum—native trees—perhaps to celebrate the architectural transformation, perhaps to break up the monolithic facade of the house.

For their 1937 Christmas card, the Freemans used an aerial photograph of Wave Hill House. In the photograph the lawn on the east side of the house has many more trees than grow there today. The land between the house and the river is more open. The north woods

Photograph for Christmas card of Edward and Dorothy Freeman. 1937. Photograph Wave Hill Archives

is a meadow, and below it, in what is today the wooded, vine-infested "disturbed" land of Riverdale Park, are several large tracts of well-tended cultivated fields. The river is not shown in the picture, and without the house to give the location its identity the place would be unrecognizable.

The history of Wave Hill, the public place, begins in 1937 with the construction of the Henry Hudson Bridge and Parkway by Robert Moses, New York City's master builder and public developer. The bridge and parkway linked Manhattan to the crest of the Riverdale ridge. The approach to the bridge from the south sweeps up through Inwood Park and over the boat canal at Spuyten Duyvil. Six to eight thousand trees in the path of the bridge were removed from the park in a single day, by almost as many workers. The bridge provides a direct auto route to Manhattan, from a place that was once a far corner of the city reachable only by a roundabout route over the escarpment from Broadway. The bridge opened on December 12, 1937, and suddenly Riverdale was fewer than fifteen miles on a straight highway along the river's edge to Forty-second Street.

Moses had accomplished what the Department of Street Improvement had been unable to do. The postwar building boom followed, and Riverdale was opened to developers. These developers were looking not for rectangular city blocks but for larger tracts of land on which to build high-rise housing complexes. Riverdale's big estates were ideal. The battle lines were drawn, this time over zoning.

As a result of a strong local movement to save this site, in 1960 the Perkins and Freeman families donated the property to the City of New York. At first it was operated as a city park known as Perkins's Gardens. Then it was established as a city-owned cultural institution, to be operated for the city by a private, non-profit corporation. The form of partnership consisting of public ownership and private management had been created in the 1890s, when the city planners decided the growing city should have great cultural institutions but should not operate them.

The transitions from private estate to park to cultural institution took five years. In 1965 Wave Hill began in earnest to seek its niche in the New York City cultural community. The gardens and environmental education were first among its priorities. During the transition period the gardens had been neglected—neglect that had obliterated all but the hardiest, weediest plants. This was the state of things when the horticulture department began its work in early 1968.

The garden at the highest point on the property, once Mrs. Perkins's spring garden, now Wave Hill's Wild Garden, had been taken over by a dozen species of rank weeds. Its major beds passed the summer of 1971 under sheets of black plastic to bake them clean. Today, more than a thousand species and varieties are carefully tended.

To discover this place is to find it filled with meticulous care for small wonders. Originally the site of a servants' house and vegetable garden, the Wild Garden is supported by dry stone retaining walls on its western and southern borders. Looking west from the garden across the river to the Palisades is like discovering the world anew. One is first aware of the steepness of the slope (the garden is 250 feet above the level of the river), the width of the river, the immensity of the cliffs beyond, and of the sky. Only then do the shapes of the foreground come into focus. The first of these are the contorted branches of a staghorn sumac and a columnar fastigiate pine, which frame the view. The nearby yews and conifers, the pergola, and the shape of this hilltop establish the limits of the garden and create a sheltering edge between it and the vast wildness of the view beyond.

This is a garden made for this particular hillside, a foil for this view. It is in humanized contrast to the stark and vast expanse of the river and the cliffs. The garden is naturalistic, but the work of generations of gardeners is represented here. In contrast to the "humanless" natural vista, this garden is tame, yet it is filled with life forms sampled from the wild.

By the early 1970s, the institution had begun to experiment with various art programs, exhibitions, and concerts. Late in the decade, the cultural institutions in the city entered a period of growth. At Wave Hill new disciplines and programs were added in the visual arts, archaeology, Hudson River studies, landscape history, forest management, and performing arts.

In 1987, as it grew toward the limits of its land and buildings, Wave Hill began a period of self-study and consolidation focused on a "mission"—to discover what unified the institution. This involved taking a fresh look at the nature of the work being done at Wave Hill and at the work being done at other places involved in the same disciplines and similar issues.

During this process Wave Hill discovered that the nature of its work had changed since 1980. These changes appeared to be similar to, or at least sympathetic with, changes that were occurring elsewhere. Many members of the staff would return to Wave Hill from conferences elated with the discovery that they were part of new movements within their fields.

For example, when Wave Hill established a program in the history of American landscape design in 1980, its goals were to foster and support the development of this new subfield of American history, to help it grow strong enough to support a comprehensive record of, and finders' guide to, landscape records. The model for this guide had been successfully established for architectural records a few years earlier. By 1988 response to the Wave Hill Catalog of Landscape Records was overwhelming. It was a classic example of an idea whose time was right. It had become a kind of national movement; professionals and enthusiasts—throughout the country, in every state—were interested in learning more about the human histories of their land and were willing and eager to volunteer their time to contribute

what they had learned to the Catalog for use by others. As interest in landscape history grew, so did awareness of the importance of cultural landscapes, and, at this writing, Congressional action is being sought to enable cultural landscapes to be designated as official national landmarks.

The Wave Hill archaeologists bucked the fashion of most city archaeologists and involved the public in their work. Education was the only strategy they felt could protect the cultural resources they were finding. Trained volunteers helped save material that would have been lost to erosion. They found support from others around the country involved in prehistoric archaeology who were working with the public and training volunteers and pursuing the same strategy for the same reasons.

When it began in 1980, Wave Hill's forest management program was sometimes described as the restoration of a remnant of the original Hudson Valley forest. However, restoration of the "original forest" was an unattainable goal. Not only did it beg the question of which forest, and at what stage in its evolution, it also ignored the chemical and biological reality of the changes that had occurred in the climate and soils and the extinction of

View of the east facade of Wave Hill House. 1990.

Photograph © Gretchen McHugh

species (American elm and chestnut) that had once been important components of this forest. Working in an urban woodland, the staff was confronted with an environment that had been dramatically altered from that for which traditional forestry schools teach management. The conventional wisdom at the time was that the best way to restore nature was leave it alone; however, left alone, the Wave Hill woods were losing their diversity of flora and fauna and becoming an unpleasant place to walk. The shrubs that grew in the locust woods around the tupelo had become a rank growth of escaped garden plants, which were obliterating the natural diversity of the native flora. What were the goals of the Wave Hill management program to be?

Around the country others were asking the same kinds of questions about formerly natural land they were seeking to restore. The new field of restoration ecology was emerging. And when the Wave Hill staff first met these restoration ecologists, everyone was mildly surprised to discover that Wave Hill's forest management program was one of the oldest active urban forest management programs in the nation, a "mature" example of a restoration-ecology project.

There was a commonality of thought to the questions Wave Hill staff asked and then discovered others were asking, to the work Wave Hill was doing and then discovered others were doing. This commonality had to do with the interaction between the realms of nature and humanity.

The issue behind these new questions was not the rights of nature in opposition to the rights of humanity but how extensively these two universes were interacting and to what extent the consequences of this interaction might explain the nature of the world we experience. These were issues that helped the Wave Hill staff to analyze, interpret, and explain what they were doing. The experience of understanding Wave Hill as a cultural landscape, it appeared, could be applied to one's experience of the world. When these were tried with the public, they seemed to work. Furthermore, these ideas created a sense of unity and purpose and an explanation for the ways in which Wave Hill had become different from other public institutions.

As a result, Wave Hill now plans its activities as extensions of a single aim: to explore and demonstrate the dynamic relationships that occur between natural processes and human culture.

View of Wave Hill House from the southwest. 1990. Photograph © Gretchen McHugh

As programs to express the mission were developed, its effectiveness became increasingly apparent. The dance program at Wave Hill was begun in order to offer works created for the land on which they were performed. Dances were commissioned for specific hillsides and lawns. Suddenly, these performances became evocations of sacred ceremonies, celebrations of place—not just any place but *this* place. It was an example of the process Wave Hill was attempting to explore, a process that is also reflected in this book.

The mission did not change Wave Hill's gardens, but it did provide a new perspective from which to view them and a way to understand the emphasis on aesthetics, which had been a powerful force in their development. The plant collections at Wave Hill are large and comprehensive. The gardens and greenhouses had become among the most admired and respected in the region, if not in America. Gardeners and garden writers understood what Wave Hill's gardens were; they had often been described as "the gardener's garden." The gardens and grounds had been planted not as displays for botanical and horticultural collections but as one would landscape a private estate. The greenhouses and gardens had been used to "teach" ecology and natural history, but they were not well suited for teaching traditional botanical-garden or nature-center curricula. For example, the cactus room in the greenhouse complex contains a fascinating collection of beautifully grown plants but does not provide the necessary environment for a study of desert ecology. Over the years, a number of ideas to improve the presentation of the gardens and to adapt them for the kinds of curricula that other public institutions taught were discussed, tried, and rejected as inappropriate to the tradition out of which Wave Hill's gardens and plant collection had been developed.

The problem was that there were no models to follow. Botanical gardens taught about the world of plants and about humanity's dependence on plants. Nature centers taught about the world of nature, most often in terms of a universe to be protected from humanity. Historic restorations reproduced gardens from the past. Wave Hill's was a contemporary garden in a historic location. With the possible exception of bonsai gardens, there were no museums that displayed living plants as objects of art. There were no botanical gardens or nature centers in which the aesthetic experience was the primary "teaching" experience. There were no public institutions that had been established to examine and demonstrate the relationships that occur between human culture and natural processes.

Nor had Wave Hill been established for this purpose. Its founding documents had resulted from a process that had preserved it from development and left vague and open ended any definition of the purposes for which it was to be used. In attempting to find a purpose Wave Hill had emulated other institutions' models by teaching what they taught. As a result, instead of analyzing, interpreting, and explaining the motivations of the gardeners and reasons why these gardens were different from those at other public places, Wave Hill had been trying to use the gardens to teach the wrong lessons, to teach biology instead of art and culture. It had been using the nature trail in the rank woodland to teach about wilderness instead of about the interactions between human and natural history that this woodland so clearly illustrates.

For example, a comparison of the photograph used for the Freemans' 1937 Christmas card (p. 154) with Lois Conner's contemporary view (plate 15) makes it clear that the com-

158

position of the trees on the lawn today is as much a product of the removal of trees by chance and nature as it is of an informed planting plan. If all the trees growing there in 1937 were there today, the lawn would be a deep woods. It had been planted in profusion but has been thinned by the wind and acid rain.

Today, the line of trees halfway up the lawn consists of one of Appleton's beeches, an elm and maple that might have grown in the Morrises' field, and conifers planted to shield an aquatic garden constructed as part of the transformation of the slope by Perkins in 1910. Along the drive, opposite the front door, Appleton's lindens are interplanted with Freeman's sweet gums. Nearby are a very old black cherry, a holdover from the pre-Revolutionary forest, and a globus form of sweet gum, a gift from Wave Hill's horticulture staff eighteen years ago. Time has matured this lawn. It is no longer obvious who was responsible for each generation of planting. It looks as though this lawn might have been this way forever.

The flower garden in front of the greenhouse, originally the Perkinses' rose garden, is now a contemporary flower garden and an ideal place in which to "teach" Wave Hill's mission. Although this garden is not a restoration, it is planted to be evocative of a 1910 American flower garden and to fit the cultural history of this landscape. In designing this garden, a series of slim volumes, titled *The Little Garden* and published around 1921, was used as a guide to establish its feel and mood.[4] It is planted predominantly in cultivars, plants first found growing in gardens. Some of these are old varieties of roses, irises, peonies, and a collection of pinks, which includes varieties cultivated since the 1500s. Growing here also are contemporary varieties, some of which made their public debut in North America at Wave Hill.

The purpose of this garden is to offer the experience of a work in progress, to offer a visit to "somebody's garden." Gardening began as an effort to transform a human environment by selecting, collecting, and mixing plants to make a more beautiful and productive place. This is the source of the fascination, excitement, and wonder that keeps gardening happening in every culture. The delight a garden can offer is the preeminent experience Wave Hill attempts to reveal.

At Wave Hill, cacti are displayed in pots, as objects with intrinsic beauty. These pots are reminders that these plants were grown by "somebody." The gardens reveal the gardener. This greenhouse room full of cacti and succulents in pots is like Earth itself. No longer an independent ecosystem, the planet will be shaped by the consequences of the interactions between humanity and nature. This room reflects the relationships—between the cacti and the gardener, between nature and the garden—that join the fate of humanity with the fate of the Earth.

Peter H. Sauer
Wave Hill, 1990

NOTES

1. Historic dates and Wave Hill facts are from two unpublished research papers written for Wave Hill by Regina M. Kellerman, in 1970, and revised and expanded by Ellen DeNooyer, in 1978.
2. From a letter written by Samuel Langhorne Clemens from Holbrook Hall, in Clara Clemens, *My Father, Mark Twain* (New York: AMS Press, 1974), 223.
3. Ibid., 228–29.
4. Francis King. *The Little Garden* (Boston: Atlantic Monthly Press, 1921).

Horticultural Diagrams

Several plants of special interest have been identified in the following thirteen diagrams made from the photographers' plates. The plant identifications are provided by Marco Polo Stufano, Wave Hill's Director of Horticulture. The line drawings are by Kelley Graphics.

Lois Conner

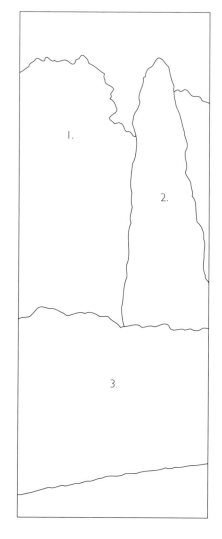

East Border Wall

PLATE SIXTEEN

1. *Juniperus chinensis* 'Spartan'

2. *Juniperus chinensis* 'Columnaris Glauca'

3. *Jasminum nudiflorum* (Winter Flowering Jasmine)

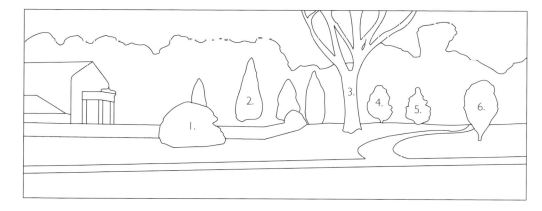

Flower Garden

1. *Acer palmatum* 'Dissectum Atropurpureum'
2. *Chamaecyparis* and *Juniperus* varieties
3. *Ulmus americana* (American Elm)
4. *Magnolia* × *Loebneri* 'Dr. Merrill'
5. *Pinus flexilis glauca* (Limber Pine)
6. *Acer griseum* (Paperbark Maple)

North Lawn

PLATE FIFTEEN

1. *Fagus sylvatica* 'Atropunicea' (European Purple Beech)
2. *Liquidambar Styraciflua* (Sweet Gum)
3. *Ulmus americana* (American Elm)
4. *Prunus serotina* (Wild Black Cherry)

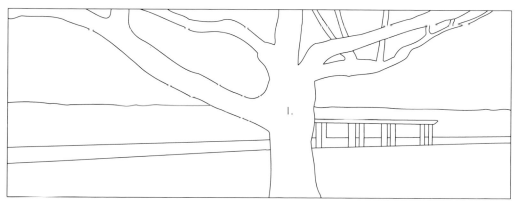

Pergola Lawn

PLATE EIGHTEEN

1. *Cladrastis lutea* (Yellowwood)

Philip Trager

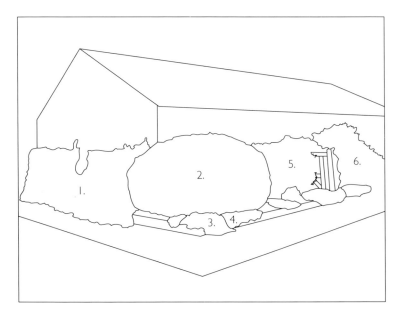

Exterior Tropical Greenhouse

PLATE TWENTY-FOUR

1. *Cotoneaster apiculatus* (Cranberry Cotoneaster)

2. *Pinus pumila* (Dwarf Stone Pine)

3. *Lobularia maritima* (Sweet Alyssum)

4. *Veronica incana*

5. *Juniperus scopulorum* 'Tabletop Blue'

6. *Picea pungens* 'Glauca Globosa' (Dwarf Blue Spruce)

Flower Garden

PLATE TWENTY-EIGHT

1. *Juniperus chinensis* 'Pfitzerana Glauca'

2. *Juniperus scopulorum* 'Grey Gleam'

3. *Juniperus occidentalis* 'Sierra Silver'

4. *Abies concolor* (White Fir)

5. *Chamaecyparis Lawsoniana* 'Erecta Blom'

6. *Juniperus scopulorum* 'Hillborn's Silver Globe'

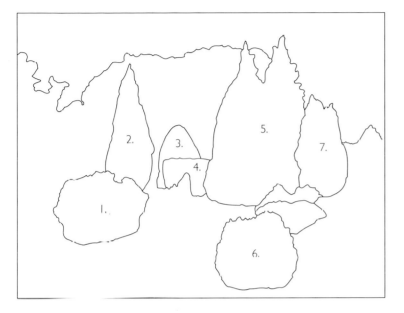

Wild Garden

PLATE THIRTY

1. *Fothergilla Gardenii*

2. *Juniperus scopulorum* 'Wichita Blue'

3. *Thuja occidentalis* 'Globosa'

4. *Cedrus Deodara* 'Pendula' (Weeping Blue Atlas Cedar)

5. *Chamaecyparis Lawsoniana* 'Wisselii'

6. *Pinus sylvestris* 'Nana' (Dwarf Scot's Pine)

7. *Chamaeyparis Lawsoniana* 'Fletcheri'

Wild Garden

PLATE THIRTY-ONE

1. *Juniperus chinensis* 'Gold Coast'

2. *Ulmus americana* (American Elm)

3. *Thuja occidentalis* 'Globosa'

4. *Cedrus Deodara* 'Pendula' (Weeping Blue Atlas Cedar)

5. *Cotoneaster conspicuus decorus*

Jan Groover

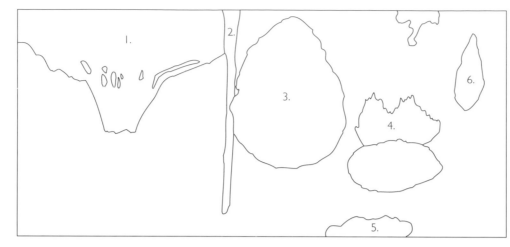

Wild Garden

PLATE FORTY-FOUR

1. *Acer Ginnala* (Amur Maple)
2. *Betula Jacquemontii*
3. *Ipomoea cultivar* (Morning Glory)
4. *Cytisus × praecox* (Warminster Broom)
5. *Bergenia cordifolia*
6. *Juniperus scopulorum* 'Wichita Blue'

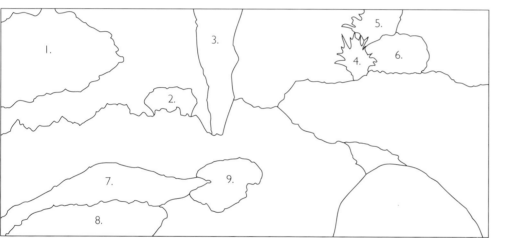

Wild Garden

PLATE FORTY-SIX

1. *Rhus typhina* 'Laciniata' (Cutleaf Staghorn Sumac)
2. *Sedum* 'Autumn Joy'
3. *Pinus Flexilis* 'Fastigiata' (Fastigiate Limber Pine)
4. *Yucca pendula*
5. *Miscanthus sinensis* 'Silver Feather'
6. *Miscanthus sinensis* 'Variegatus'
7. *Juniperus chinensis procumbens* 'Nana'
8. *Cerastium tomentosum* (Snow in Summer)
9. *Buxus microphylla* 'Compacta' (Dwarf Box)

Wild Garden

PLATE FIFTY

1. *Gaura Lindheimeri*
2. *Yucca pendula*
3. *Cotoneaster horizontalis*
4. *Miscanthus sinensis* 'Variegatus'
5. *Platycodon grandiflorus* (Balloon Flower)
6. *Hemerocallis cultivar*
7. *Juniperus horizontalis* 'Wiltonii'

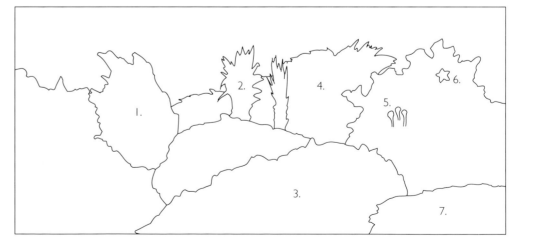

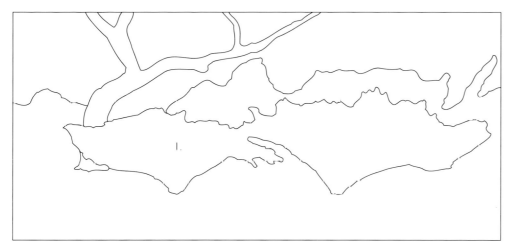

Wood's Edge

PLATE FIFTY-THREE

1. *Corylopsis platypetala* (Winter Hazel)

Interior Cactus Greenhouse

PLATE FIFTY-SEVEN

1. *Opuntia Tuna*
2. *Mammillaria* sp.
3. *Espostoa* sp.
4. *Agave* sp.
5. × *Pachyveria glauca*
6. × *Graptoveria* 'Fanfare'
7. *Opuntia Lindheimeri var. linguiformis*
8. *Echeveria* 'Harry Butterfield'
9. *Notocactus Leninghaussii*

Index
of Plates

The photographers have elected to list their pictures as untitled; therefore, the photographs are identified by the artists' own negative numbers. Jan Groover and Philip Trager worked at Wave Hill from fall 1987 through early 1989. Lois Conner and Stephen A. Scheer photographed during 1989.

Lois Conner